# Everyone's Introduction To Bridge Conventions

*Other Avon Books by*
**Shelly de Satnick**

Bridge For Everyone

# EVERYONE'S INTRODUCTION TO BRIDGE CONVENTIONS

## SHELLY de SATNICK

AVON
PUBLISHERS OF BARD, CAMELOT, DISCUS AND FLARE BOOKS

EVERYONE'S INTRODUCTION TO BRIDGE CONVEN-
TIONS is an original publication of Avon Books. This work has
never before appeared in book form.

AVON BOOKS
A division of
The Hearst Corporation
1790 Broadway
New York, New York 10019

First Avon Printing, November, 1984

AVON TRADEMARK REG. U. S. PAT. OFF. AND IN
OTHER COUNTRIES, MARCA REGISTRADA, HECHO EN
U. S. A.

Printed in the U. S. A.

OPB 10 9 8 7 6 5 4 3 2 1

To my father, whom I love very much

# ACKNOWLEDGMENTS

*A special thanks to the following people without whom this book would never have been a reality:*
*George Biris*
*Willie Ross*
*Nellie Sabin*
*Trumbull Rogers*

# CONTENTS

# Introduction

This book is designed for those partnerships who have a solid foundation as taught in *Bridge For Everyone* and are now ready to add some sophistication to their game.

A *convention* takes a natural bid and gives it an artificial meaning. It asks partner for specific information or gives partner information not related to the bid itself.

Many players believe that by adopting lots of conventions they will no longer have to think. They believe that the conventions play themselves. Let me destroy that myth. When you use conventions, you have to think more. Every time you choose to play a particular convention, you give up one or more natural bids. This in itself presents a problem. In addition, the proper use of the convention can be problematic.

The conventions are listed in alphebetical order. First I discuss the purpose of each convention, then the natural bid given up, and finally the convention's advantage. Often a basic defense is offered against opponents who use a convention against you.

Admittedly, using "gadgets" is fun, and I will try to give you a sound approach to the use of some of the more popular conventions. I am not necessarily advocating the adoption of these conventions. I do, however, feel that you should have a working knowledge of them, if only to know what your opponents are doing if they use any of these conventions.

If after you adopt a convention it is not used in a particular auction, you must be aware of the negative inference. If partner does not make a conventional call when one could apply, then he must not have that particular type of hand. (Of course, at first he may have simply forgotten. This is one of the early dangers when adopting a convention!) Assume that partner did not forget and use the information during the remainder of the auction.

When your partner makes a conventional call you must alert your opponents to your private understanding. You do this by simply saying the word *alert*. At this time the opponent whose turn it is to bid may ask for an explanation. The one who alerted— the partner of the player who made the conventional call—gives the explanation. In the text, all alertable bids are followed by the word ALERTABLE in parentheses.

Choose with care the conventions you decide to use, and I suggest you adopt them one at a time. Make each one an integral part of your system before going on to the next one. I hope you get to more of the right contracts than ever before.

# One

## Astro

**Purpose:** To show two-suited hands after an opponent's opening bid of 1 N.T.

**Natural Bid Given Up:** The bids of 2♣ and 2♦ over an opponent's opening bid of 1 N.T. to show one-suited hands with clubs or diamonds.

**Advantage:** It is generally agreed that it is more profitable to compete after a strong hand is announced with a two-suited hand rather than a one-suited hand. Over an opening 1 N.T. it is difficult to show two-suited hands, since often there is not an opportunity to bid twice.

If right-hand opponent opens 1 N.T., the overcall of 2♣ (ALERTABLE) shows hearts, called the *anchor* suit, and an unspecified minor suit. The overcall of 2♦ (ALERTABLE) shows spades, the anchor suit, and another unspecified lower-ranking suit (hearts, diamonds, or clubs). The Astro bidder promises at least nine cards in his two suits and good values in the suits if vulnerable. Point count is not quite as relevant as distribution and playing strength. In direct seat you should have about 10 points in your two suits, a little more if vulnerable. This is a real judgment situation. As your suits get longer and the vulnerability is favorable, you may have fewer points.

An overcall of 2 ♥ or 2 ♠ is natural, showing a one-suited hand. You must jump to 3 ♣ or 3 ♦, however, to show one-suited minor hands. The overcall of 2 N.T. is still unusual for the minors (see p. 113).

Right-hand opponent opens 1 N.T. and you hold each of the following hands:

| a) | ♠ KQ765 | b) | ♠ 76 | c) | ♠ QJ1075 |
|---|---|---|---|---|---|
| | ♥ AJ653 | | ♥ AK743 | | ♥ 5 |
| | ♦ 5 | | ♦ QJ76 | | ♦ 93 |
| | ♣ 94 | | ♣ 32 | | ♣ AQ863 |
| | Bid 2 ♦ | | Bid 2 ♣ | | Bid 2 ♦ |
| d) | ♠ AQJ987 | e) | ♠ 9 | f) | ♠ 987 |
| | ♥ 6 | | ♥ 64 | | ♥ 54 |
| | ♦ A32 | | ♦ KJ875 | | ♦ AK |
| | ♣ 854 | | ♣ KQJ84 | | ♣ KQJ986 |
| | Bid 2 ♠ | | Bid 2 N.T. | | Bid 3 ♣ |

Astro may also be used in the balancing seat after left-hand opponent opens 1 N.T. and partner and right-hand opponent pass. In this position you may have fewer points, since partner is marked with some high-card strength.

Responding to the Astro bidder requires considerable judgment, again proving the need to think more with the adoption of a convention.

• Bid two of the anchor major with at least three cards and no game interest (0–10 points).

• Bid three of the anchor major with at least four cards (Astro bidder may have only a 4-card major) and an interest in game (11–14 points).

• Bid four of the anchor major with at least four cards and the desire to play game (15 plus points).

• You may pass with a weak hand and six cards in the bid suit.

• Bid two of the neutral suit (ALERTABLE), the next suit above the Astro bid, which is negative, denying the ability to make any other response. You must have at least two cards in the neutral suit.

• Bid 2 N.T. (ALERTABLE) forcing and artificial, showing some support for the anchor major, suggesting game without promising another bid.

• A new suit take-out or jump (including a jump in the neutral suit or a raise of the take-out suit) shows a 6-card suit and some high-card strength.

Left-hand opponent opens 1 N.T. and partner overcalls 2 ♦, Astro, showing spades and a lower-ranking suit. Right-hand opponent passes and you hold each of the following hands:

| a) | ♠ K76 | b) | ♠ AQ87 | c) | ♠ J9764 |
|----|--------|----|---------|----|----------|
|    | ♥ 876  |    | ♥ 76    |    | ♥ 5      |
|    | ♦ Q765 |    | ♦ AJ64  |    | ♦ AJ65   |
|    | ♣ 765  |    | ♣ 1086  |    | ♣ AQ6    |
|    | Bid 2 ♠ |   | Bid 3 ♠ |    | Bid 4 ♠  |

| d) | ♠ 84    | e) | ♠ 85    | f) | ♠ K87   |
|----|---------|----|---------|----|---------|
|    | ♥ 86    |    | ♥ 965   |    | ♥ A54   |
|    | ♦ KJ7653|    | ♦ Q876  |    | ♦ K875  |
|    | ♣ 532   |    | ♣ Q643  |    | ♣ Q52   |
|    | Pass    |    | Bid 2 ♥ |    | Bid 2 N.T. |

| g) | ♠ 63     | h) | ♠ 92     | i) | ♠ 92     |
|----|----------|----|----------|----|----------|
|    | ♥ AK8754 |    | ♥ A3     |    | ♥ KJ     |
|    | ♦ K4     |    | ♦ AQJ875 |    | ♦ 753    |
|    | ♣ 543    |    | ♣ 432    |    | ♣ AQJ975 |
|    | Bid 3 ♥  |    | Bid 3 ♦  |    | Bid 3 ♣  |

After a neutral response the Astro bidder has a choice of rebids.

• He may pass with five cards in the neutral suit, that being his second suit.

• He may show five cards in the anchor major by "rebidding" it.

• He may show his second suit at the three-level, indicating a 6-card suit and good playing strength.

• He may bid 2 N.T. (ALERTABLE), denying five cards in his major, but showing five cards in his other suit. This bid is forcing. The responder is now likely to bid clubs, allowing the Astro bidder to pass if clubs is his second suit or to now bid his second suit to play.

In most sequences 2 N.T. (ALERTABLE) by either player is artificial and forcing. As second bid by responder it is likely to be weak, asking for Astro bidder's second suit.

Right-hand opponent opens 1 N.T. and with each of the following hands you overcall 2♣, Astro, showing hearts and a minor. Left-hand opponent passes and partner responds 2♦, the neutral suit. Right-hand opponent passes.

| a) | ♠ A3 | b) | ♠ 74 |
|---|---|---|---|
| | ♥ KJ87 | | ♥ AQJ76 |
| | ♦ QJ1075 | | ♦ 43 |
| | ♣ 43 | | ♣ AJ65 |
| | Pass | | Rebid 2♥ |
| c) | ♠ 43 | d) | ♠ 92 |
| | ♥ AJ84 | | ♥ AK65 |
| | ♦ 5 | | ♦ 74 |
| | ♣ KQJ653 | | ♣ KQ743 |
| | Rebid 3♣ | | Rebid 2 N.T. |

In the fourth example, the rebid of 2 N.T. must show clubs since you would have passed 2♦ with five of them.

**Basic Defense:** 2 N.T. is natural inviting game. A double shows a defensive hand with a good holding in the anchor suit and the suit doubled. A cue bid of the anchor suit is game-going and shows a hand unsuited for defense. You may pass to see what happens (remember, nothing may happen). A new suit bid (non-jump), including the Astro bidder's minor, is unconstructive and nonforcing.

## *QUIZ #1*

1. Right-hand opponent opens 1 N.T. Playing Astro, what do you bid with each of the following hands?

a)
♠ KQJ76
♥ KJ632
♦ 5
♣ 94 ___

b)
♠ 83
♥ AQ986
♦ KQ76
♣ 93 ___

c)
♠ AK76
♥ 5
♦ 84
♣ AJ10864 ___

d)
♠ K8753
♥ 54
♦ J8654
♣ 5 ___

e)
♠ A3
♥ KQJ875
♦ 54
♣ 853 ___

f)
♠ 876
♥ AJ109
♦ 8
♣ KJ863 ___

g)
♠ KQ
♥ 765
♦ AQJ754
♣ 54 ___

2. Left-hand opponent opens 1 N.T. Partner overcalls 2♣ Astro. Right-hand opponent passes. What do you respond with each of the following hands?

a)
♠ Q64
♥ 54
♦ 54
♣ K76542 ___

b)
♠ A43
♥ 987
♦ Q76
♣ 9753 ___

c)
♠ KQ3
♥ A74
♦ Q543
♣ Q32 ___

d)
♠ A3
♥ AQ54
♦ 762
♣ Q876 ___

e)
♠ 9743
♥ 94
♦ 54
♣ QJ987 ___

f)
♠ 6
♥ Q9864
♦ AK5
♣ KJ62 ___

g)
♠ A32
♥ 72
♦ Q3
♣ KQJ987 ___

3. Right-hand opponent opens 1 N.T. With each of the following hands you overcall 2 ♦ Astro. Left-hand opponent passes and partner responds 2 ♥, the neutral suit. Right-hand opponent passes. What do you rebid?

a)  ♠ KJ1095          b)  ♠ AQ97
    ♥ 54                  ♥ KJ876
    ♦ KQ876              ♦ 6
    ♣ 5 ___              ♣ 954 ___

c)  ♠ AK87            d)  ♠ AK54
    ♥ 5                  ♥ 875
    ♦ 97                 ♦ 7
    ♣ AQ9863 ___         ♣ KQ865 ___

# *Two*

# Cappelletti

**Purpose:** To show a one- or two-suited hand after an opponent's opening bid of 1 N.T.

**Natural Bid Given Up:** All two-level bids over an opponent's opening 1 N.T. to show that suit.

**Advantage:** You can show any one-suited hand as well as all combinations of two-suited hands.

If right-hand opponent opens 1 N.T., an overcall of 2 ♣ (ALERTABLE) shows a one-suited hand and requires partner to bid 2 ♦. You can then pass if your suit is diamonds, or you can bid 3 ♦ if you wish to invite game. A bid of 2 ♥ or 2 ♠ shows those suits, respectively, and a bid of 3 ♥ or 3 ♠ shows those suits with a better hand and invites game. The rebid of 3 ♣ shows clubs.

Right-hand opponent opens 1 N.T. and you bid 2 ♣ with each of the following hands. Left-hand opponent passes and partner bids 2 ♦ perforce. Right-hand opponent passes.

a)  ♠ KQJ764
    ♥ 54
    ♦ K32
    ♣ 63

    Rebid 2♠

b)  ♠ A3
    ♥ AQJ543
    ♦ Q43
    ♣ 74

    Rebid 3♥

c)  ♠ 76
    ♥ K54
    ♦ QJ87543
    ♣ 9

    Pass

d)  ♠ A4
    ♥ 653
    ♦ K5
    ♣ KQ10754

    Rebid 3♣

If right-hand opponent opens 1 N.T., an overcall of 2♦ (ALERTABLE) shows at least nine cards in the major suits. Your point count varies with vulnerability and length of suits. A good guide is about 10 points not vulnerable and a little more vulnerable.

Right-hand opponent opens 1 N.T. and you hold each of the following hands:

a)  ♠ KQ876
    ♥ AJ543
    ♦ 54
    ♣ 5

    Bid 2♦

b)  ♠ J7654
    ♥ AK43
    ♦ 94
    ♣ 87

    Pass

c)  ♠ K876
    ♥ AQJ54
    ♦ Q76
    ♣ 9

    Bid 2♦

If right-hand opponent opens 1 N.T., an overcall of 2♥ (ALERTABLE) shows five hearts and at least four of an unspecified minor.

Right-hand opponent opens 1 N.T. and you hold each of the following hands:

| a) | ♠ 76 | b) | ♠ 9 | c) | ♠ 843 |
|---|---|---|---|---|---|
| | ♥ KQ875 | | ♥ AJ953 | | ♥ K8764 |
| | ♦ AJ542 | | ♦ 754 | | ♦ Q7653 |
| | ♣ 9 | | ♣ AKQ3 | | ♣ — |
| | Bid 2♥ | | Bid 2♥ | | Pass |

If right-hand opponent opens 1 N.T., an overcall of 2♠ (ALERTABLE) shows five spades and at least four of an unspecified minor.

Right-hand opponent opens 1 N.T. and you hold each of the following hands:

| a) | ♠ KJ1095 | b) | ♠ AKJ43 | c) | ♠ 97543 |
|---|---|---|---|---|---|
| | ♥ 5 | | ♥ 65 | | ♥ K |
| | ♦ KQJ64 | | ♦ 96 | | ♦ Q9754 |
| | ♣ 74 | | ♣ AQ85 | | ♣ AJ |
| | Bid 2♠ | | Bid 2♠ | | Pass |

Cappelletti can be used in the direct seat and or in the balancing seat. It can be used over weak or strong no trump opening bids. Be sure to discuss which way you are going to play it with your partner.

If right-hand opponent opens 1 N.T., an overcall of 2 N.T. asks for the minors. See Unusual No Trump (page 111).

If left-hand opponent opens 1 N.T. and partner bids 2♣, Cappelletti, you are forced to bid 2♦. However, with a good six-card suit of your own, you may bid that suit.

Left-hand opponent opens 1 N.T., partner bids 2♣, right-hand opponent passes and you hold the following hands:

| a) | ♠ K854 | b) | ♠ 86 | c) | ♠ AQ754 |
|---|---|---|---|---|---|
| | ♥ 65 | | ♥ AQJ986 | | ♥ 765 |
| | ♦ Q75 | | ♦ 65 | | ♦ 85 |
| | ♣ 9743 | | ♣ 965 | | ♣ 954 |
| | Bid 2♦ | | Bid 2♥ | | Bid 2♦ |

If left-hand opponent opens 1 N.T. and partner bids 2♦, asking for a major, choose to respond in your longer major. You respond at the two-level with no interest in game, at the three-level with game interest (11–15 points), and may even bid game.

Left-hand opponent opens 1 N.T., partner bids 2♦, right-hand opponent passes, and you hold each of the following hands:

| a) | ♠ 987 | b) | ♠ A9 | c) | ♠ K754 |
|---|---|---|---|---|---|
| | ♥ 65 | | ♥ K876 | | ♥ A8765 |
| | ♦ KJ76 | | ♦ KQ54 | | ♦ A43 |
| | ♣ QJ43 | | ♣ J54 | | ♣ 9 |
| | Bid 2♠ | | Bid 3♥ | | Bid 4♥ |

If left-hand opponent opens 1 N.T. and partner overcalls a major suit, you can pass, if you like partner's major and have no interest in game. You may raise partner's suit with a good hand (11–15 points) and interest in game. If you have shortness in partner's major and wish to know which minor suit he has, you bid 2 N.T. (ALERTABLE), which is artificial and asks partner to bid his minor suit.

Left-hand opponent opens 1 N.T., partner overcalls 2♥, right-hand opponent passes, and you hold each of the following hands:

| a) ♠ 87 | b) ♠ A4 | c) ♠ 984 |
|---|---|---|
| ♥ K84 | ♥ 9876 | ♥ 52 |
| ♦ Q432 | ♦ AK42 | ♦ QJ65 |
| ♣ 9743 | ♣ 654 | ♣ KJ74 |
| Pass | Bid 3♥ | Bid 2 N.T. |

## QUIZ #2

**1.** Right-hand opponent opens 1 N.T. Playing Cappelletti, what do you bid with each of the following hands?

| a) ♠ KQJ854 | b) ♠ KJ732 | c) ♠ A4 |
|---|---|---|
| ♥ A5 | ♥ AQ953 | ♥ KJ642 |
| ♦ 954 | ♦ 8 | ♦ AQ965 |
| ♣ 83 ___ | ♣ 94 ___ | ♣ 6 ___ |

| d) ♠ AQ954 | e) ♠ 854 |
|---|---|
| ♥ 4 | ♥ KJ6 |
| ♦ 105 | ♦ AQ10853 |
| ♣ AK1085 ___ | ♣ 7 ___ |

**2.** Left-hand opponent opens 1 N.T. Playing Cappelletti, what do you respond with each of the following hands if partner overcalls 1) 2♣; 2) 2♦; 3) 2♥; and 4) 2♠?

a)  ♠ KJ64
    ♥ Q75
    ♦ 987
    ♣ 643        1. ___   2. ___   3. ___   4. ___

b)  ♠ A8
    ♥ 943
    ♦ Q853
    ♣ Q953       1. ___   2. ___   3. ___   4. ___

c)  ♠ KQ65
    ♥ A8
    ♦ QJ93
    ♣ 965        1. ___   2. ___   3. ___   4. ___

# *Three*

# Dope, Dopi

**Purpose:** To be able to show the number of aces you have if partner bids Blackwood and the opponents interfere.

**Natural Bid Given Up:** The ability to double the interference bid for penalty.

**Advantage:** Even though the opponents interfere, your slam may depend on the number of aces the partnership holds. Using one of these conventions, you can still show how many aces you have.

If partner bids 4 N.T., Blackwood, and right-hand opponent bids at the five-level, playing DOPE, a double shows an odd number of aces (1 or 3); pass shows an even number (0, 2, or 4). Therefore, the letters DOPE stand for *d*ouble *o*dd, *p*ass *e*ven. The Blackwood user can usually figure out which it is.

If you are playing DOPI, you double with no aces and pass with one. Therefore, the letters DOPI stand for *d*ouble with *none* (0) and *p*ass with *one* (1). Holding two or more aces you use step responses. The next suit above the interference suit shows two aces, the next suit three aces, etc.

## *QUIZ #3*

1. Partner bids 4 N.T., Blackwood, and right-hand opponent overcalls 5♣. What do you respond a) Playing DOPE? b) Playing DOPI?

a)
♠ A765
♥ KJ5
♦ QJ54
♣ 54 ___ ___

b)
♠ KQ65
♥ KQ76
♦ K5
♣ Q94 ___ ___

c)
♠ A964
♥ AQ432
♦ 54
♣ 92 ___ ___

d)
♠ AJ65
♥ A54
♦ A3
♣ 8642 ___ ___

# *Four*

# Drury

**Purpose:** To find out whether partner's third- or fourth-seat major-suit opening is "light" or based on a full 13 or more points.

**Natural Bid Given Up:** The response of 2♣ to show clubs.

**Advantage:** To keep from jumping as a passed hand with close to an opening bid and perhaps being a level too high if partner opened subminimum.

If partner opens a major suit in third or fourth position, the response of 2♣ (ALERTABLE) is artificial, asking the opener whether he has full values for his opening bid. If the opener is subminimum, he rebids 2♦ (ALERTABLE), also artificial, warning responder that he opened "light." Any other rebid shows a full opening bid and is natural.

Partner opens 1♠ in third seat. With each of the following hands you respond 2♣ Drury:

| a) | ♠ Q987 | b) | ♠ 1096 |
|---|---|---|---|
| | ♥ A765 | | ♥ A4 |
| | ♦ K7 | | ♦ KJ63 |
| | ♣ QJ4 | | ♣ K963 |

If opener rebids 2 ♦, showing a subminimum hand, you rebid only 2 ♠, which shows a stronger hand than if you had responded 2 ♠ directly.

The responder does not necessarily guarantee a fit in the opened major. He would bid Drury with each of the following hands, too:

| a) | ♠ J6 | b) | ♠ 9 |
|---|---|---|---|
| | ♥ KQ65 | | ♥ QJ4 |
| | ♦ K53 | | ♦ 852 |
| | ♣ K754 | | ♣ AQJ753 |

With hand a), the responder can avoid bidding 2 N.T., which may be too high if partner opened light. Using Drury can also help find a heart fit if the opener also has four hearts. Respond 2 ♣, Drury. If partner rebids 2 ♦, showing a light opening bid, you now rebid 2 ♥, showing a 4-card suit. If opener rebids anything else, he shows a full opening bid and the responder can rebid accordingly.

With hand b), the responder bids 2 ♣, followed by 3 ♣.

The opener's rebid of 2 ♦ is not always negative and cannot be passed. He may have a full opening bid, with diamonds as his second suit. If this is the case, he follows with a constructive bid of 2 N.T. or a bid at the three-level, which enables the responder to make a decision.

With each of the following hands, you open 1 ♠ in third position. Partner responds 2 ♣, Drury, and you rebid 2 ♦. Partner then bids 2 ♠.

| a) | ♠ KQ765 | b) | ♠ KQ843 | c) | ♠ KQ843 |
|---|---|---|---|---|---|
|  | ♥ 65 |  | ♥ K3 |  | ♥ A32 |
|  | ♦ AKJ63 |  | ♦ QJ54 |  | ♦ J4 |
|  | ♣ 4 |  | ♣ A3 |  | ♣ 843 |

With hand a), you should now rebid 3 ♦ , showing your distribution and a full opening bid.

With hand b), you should rebid 2 N.T., showing a full opening and a hand suited for no trump as well as spades.

With hand c), you should pass, since your 2 ♦ bid was, in fact, negative.

**Basic Defense:**   The double of 2 ♣ , Drury, shows clubs.

## *QUIZ #4*

**1.** Partner opens 1 ♠ in third seat. Playing Drury, what do you respond with each of the following hands?

| a) | ♠ QJ76 | b) | ♠ 93 | c) | ♠ 9876 |
|---|---|---|---|---|---|
|  | ♥ K43 |  | ♥ AQ87 |  | ♥ KQ5 |
|  | ♦ A432 |  | ♦ K76 |  | ♦ Q76 |
|  | ♣ J4 ___ |  | ♣ QJ84 ___ |  | ♣ 954 ___ |

| d) | ♠ AQ874 | e) | ♠ 85 |
|---|---|---|---|
|  | ♥ — |  | ♥ 84 |
|  | ♦ K432 |  | ♦ K65 |
|  | ♣ Q543 ___ |  | ♣ AK10985 ___ |

**2.** With each of the following hands, you open 1♠ in third seat. Partner responds 2♣, Drury. What do you rebid?

a)   ♠ KQJ76       b)   ♠ KJ543       c)   ♠ AKJ74
    ♥ 432           ♥ A432           ♥ A3
    ♦ AJ3           ♦ 43           ♦ Q94
    ♣ 84 ___           ♣ AQ ___           ♣ 843 ___

d)   ♠ QJ864       e)   ♠ AQ852
    ♥ KJ3           ♥ AJ74
    ♦ QJ10           ♦ 92
    ♣ A4 ___           ♣ 106 ___

# *Five*

# Flannery 2 ♦

**Purpose:** To handle opening hands with four spades and five hearts and not enough points (17 or more) to reverse the bidding.

**Natural Bid Given Up:** Opening 2 ♦ preemptive, assuming that you are playing weak two bids.

**Advantage:** Those who adopt Flannery feel that the weak 2 ♦ bid is the least preemptive, since either major suit can be bid by an opponent at the two level. Being able to show your point count and major suit distribution with one bid, thus eliminating an awkward rebid after opening 1 ♥ if partner responds two of a minor, justifies playing Flannery.

The opening bid of 2 ♦ (ALERTABLE), after agreeing with your partner to play Flannery, will show a hand with four spades, five hearts, and 11 to a bad 16 high-card points. Your minor-suit distribution is undetermined except for the fact that you have only four cards in the minor suits.

The following are hands with which you will open 2 ♦, Flannery:

| a) | ♠ AJ87 | b) | ♠ KQ63 | c) | ♠ AQ74 |
|---|---|---|---|---|---|
| | ♥ KQ753 | | ♥ A8732 | | ♥ KJ852 |
| | ♦ Q8 | | ♦ A43 | | ♦ — |
| | ♣ 63 | | ♣ 9 | | ♣ K874 |

When opening Flannery with the lower point range (11–13), most of your points should be in the major suits. Why look for trouble?

Responding to Flannery is more complicated than opening Flannery. The responder can place the final contract or can ask the opener for more information. He can ask whether opener is minimum or maximum, or he can get more information about his minor-suit holding. First let's discuss responder's placing the contract.

The response of 2 ♥ or 2 ♠ denies the values for game and requests that the opener pass. These bids do not guarantee a fit, since responder may simply be choosing the lesser of two evils.

Partner opens 2 ♦, Flannery, and you hold each of the following hands:

| a) | ♠ K5 | b) | ♠ QJ53 | c) | ♠ 98 |
|---|---|---|---|---|---|
| | ♥ Q74 | | ♥ 95 | | ♥ 84 |
| | ♦ Q864 | | ♦ K74 | | ♦ K762 |
| | ♣ 9742 | | ♣ K852 | | ♣ Q8643 |
| | Respond 2 ♥ | | Respond 2 ♠ | | Respond 2 ♥ |

The response of 4 ♥ or 4 ♠ also places the final contract and shows the values for game.

Partner opens 2 ♦, Flannery, and you hold each of the following hands:

**a)**  ♠ K876        **b)**  ♠ 754
      ♥ 76                 ♥ K95
      ♦ AK74               ♦ A743
      ♣ QJ2                ♣ KQJ

   Respond 4♠            Respond 4♥

The response of 3 N.T. is to play. It shows an opening bid and stoppers in both minors.

Partner opens 2 ♦, Flannery, and you hold each of the following hands:

**a)**  ♠ Q65         **b)**  ♠ 92
      ♥ 92                 ♥ 64
      ♦ AQ86               ♦ AKQJ6
      ♣ AJ103              ♣ K542

   Respond 3 N.T.        Respond 3 N.T.

The responses of 4♣ or 4♦ are transfers. 4♣ (ALERTABLE) transfers to 4♥, and 4♦ (ALERTABLE) transfers to 4♠. These bids should be used when you have no tenace positions in the minor suits and feel the opening lead should come to partner's hand.

Partner opens 2♦, Flannery, and you hold each of the following hands:

**a)**  ♠ K874        **b)**  ♠ 876
      ♥ Q2                 ♥ AK3
      ♦ A86                ♦ QJ109
      ♣ A432               ♣ A43

   Respond 4♦            Respond 4♣

Now let's discuss asking bids. The response of 3 ♥ or 3 ♠ is invitational, requiring 10–12 points, and asks opener to pass with a minimum and to accept game with a maximum (11–13 high-card points is considered minimum, and 14–16 high-card points maximum).

Partner opens 2 ♦, Flannery, and you hold each of the following hands:

| a) | ♠ K854 | b) | ♠ 98 |
|---|---|---|---|
| | ♥ Q3 | | ♥ Q543 |
| | ♦ A85 | | ♦ QJ86 |
| | ♣ Q973 | | ♣ AQ7 |
| | Respond 3 ♠ | | Respond 3 ♥ |

We now discuss the bids that ask the opener specific information about his minor-suit distribution. Having a hand with the values for game, no 8-card fit in either major, and one of the minor suits unprotected presents a real problem.

Partner opens 2 ♦ and you hold:

♠ A74 ♥ 85 ♦ AKQJ ♣ 9743. If partner has a club stopper, you would like to play 3 N.T. Therefore, the response of three of a minor (ALERTABLE) asks opener to bid 3 N.T. with a *stopper* in that minor. With the above hand, you respond 3 ♣. If partner rebids 3 N.T., showing a club stopper, you pass. If the opener does not have a stopper in the minor suit asked about, he returns to 3 ♥ so that the responder can place the contract. This is not always so easy for the responder. With the hand in question, if partner rebids 3 ♥, you should bid 4 ♥. You know that partner has two good suits since he has no club stopper and can have no values in diamonds. Why the 7-card heart fit rather than the 7-card spade fit? If partner is short in clubs (the suit the opponents will assuredly lead), he will have to trump the suit and can handle the pump in hearts holding five of them. If partner has to lose three club tricks, he may still be able to pull trump and get rid of any spade losers on the diamonds. (Here is a perfect example of how the adoption of a convention *does not* eliminate the need to think!)

The other asking bid the responder has available with which to ask about minor suits is 2 N.T. This bid is used mostly when you have an interest in slam and a fit in one of partner's major suits. The bid of 2 N.T. (ALERTABLE) is artificial and asks the opener about his minor suit *distribution*.

If the opener is 3–1 or 1–3 in the minors, he rebids his 3-card minor at the three-level (ALERTABLE) regardless of its high-card content. Since the opener can have only four cards in the minor suits, this rebid shows a singleton in the other minor.

With the following hand: ♠AJ86 ♥KQJ87 ♦A63 ♣7 you open 2♦, Flannery. Partner responds 2 N.T., and you rebid 3♦. Now let's take a look at responder's hand. He bid 2 N.T., holding: ♠KQ53 ♥A7 ♦KQJ6 ♣963. When you rebid 3♦, partner knows that you have a singleton club and that every card in the two hands is "working." The responder can now bid 4 N.T. (Blackwood), and when you show two aces, will carry on to 6♠, knowing you have an excellent chance of making it. With the actual cards (and only 30 high-card points), the slam is cold with no worse than a 4–1 spade break.

If the opener is 4–0 or 0–4 in the minors, after responder bids 2 N.T., he rebids his 4-card minor at the four-level (ALERTABLE). This, of course, shows a void in the other minor.

With the following hand: ♠KQ74 ♥AK953 ♦— ♣K963 you open 2♦, Flannery. Partner responds 2 N.T., and you rebid 4♣. Now let's take a look at responder's hand. He bid 2 N.T.

holding: ♠ A4 ♥ QJ643 ♦ 975 ♣ AQ7. Knowing you have a void in diamonds, responder now bids 4 N.T., and you show one ace (obviously the ♥ A). He then bids 5 N.T., and when you show three kings, it's a simple matter to bid the lay-down grand slam in hearts with only 28 high-card points. (Let's hear it for Flannery!)

None of the minor-suit asking bids tells you whether opener is minimum or maximum. You can't have everything.

If the opener is 4–5–2–2, he responds to the asking bid of 2 N.T. in one of the following ways. He rebids 3 ♥ (ALERT-ABLE) with a minimum (11–13 high-card points) and 3 ♠ (ALERTABLE) with a maximum (15 or 16 high-card points). With 14 points, you must exercise judgment. Treat a bad 14 as minimum and a good 14 as maximum.

With 4-5-2-2 distribution, a maximum, and a queen or better in *each* of the minors, rebid 3 N.T. (ALERTABLE).

With each of the following hands, you open 2 ♦ , Flannery, and partner responds 2 N.T.

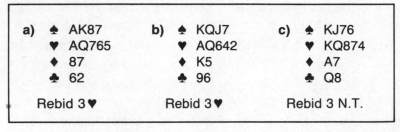

| a) | ♠ AK87 | b) | ♠ KQJ7 | c) | ♠ KJ76 |
|---|---|---|---|---|---|
|  | ♥ AQ765 |  | ♥ AQ642 |  | ♥ KQ874 |
|  | ♦ 87 |  | ♦ K5 |  | ♦ A7 |
|  | ♣ 62 |  | ♣ 96 |  | ♣ Q8 |
|  | Rebid 3 ♥ |  | Rebid 3 ♥ |  | Rebid 3 N.T. |

The responder can pass the opening bid of 2 ♦ if he holds six or more diamonds and has no fit for either of partner's majors. This is rare and usually the color drains from partner's face—which, incidentally, will return as you score it up for a par result.

**Basic Defense:** If the right-hand opponent opens 2♦, Flannery, a double shows diamonds for lead direction or a possible place to sacrifice if the opponents get to four of a major. The bid of 3♦ shows diamonds and a good hand.

## QUIZ #5

1. Playing Flannery, what do you open with each of the following hands?

a)
♠ K876
♥ AQJ76
♦ K4
♣ 76 ___

b)
♠ KQJ75
♥ A765
♦ A54
♣ 9 ___

c)
♠ Q876
♥ J7643
♦ A3
♣ KJ ___

d)
♠ AQ76
♥ AKQ76
♦ A6
♣ 32 ___

e)
♠ AQ87
♥ AJ1098
♦ 743
♣ 6 ___

f)
♠ KJ65
♥ KQJ32
♦ K3
♣ A2 ___

2. Partner opens 2♦, Flannery. What do you respond with each of the following hands?

a)
♠ K876
♥ Q7
♦ J864
♣ 864 ___

b)
♠ 65
♥ Q876
♦ AQJ
♣ KJ85 ___

c)
♠ A976
♥ 65
♦ KQ54
♣ Q75 ___

d)
♠ AK43
♥ Q43
♦ AKQ3
♣ 43 ___

e)
♠ 754
♥ Q3
♦ AK65
♣ AQ42 ___

f)
♠ AK54
♥ 98
♦ A63
♣ QJ109 ___

g)
♠ 97
♥ 5
♦ AQ8643
♣ 8643 ___

h)
♠ 65
♥ Q3
♦ Q8754
♣ Q542 ___

3. With each of the following hands, you opened 2 ♦ , Flannery, partner responded 2 N.T. What do you rebid?

a) ♠ KJ87  b) ♠ AQ87  c) ♠ AK96
   ♥ AQ765    ♥ KQJ76    ♥ QJ654
   ♦ 54       ♦ 543      ♦ K753
   ♣ Q2 ___   ♣ 4 ___    ♣ — ___

d) ♠ KQ76  e) ♠ A765
   ♥ AQJ76    ♥ KJ765
   ♦ K4       ♦ A3
   ♣ 54 ___   ♣ Q8 ___

4. ♠ KQ54      Your hand is at left. You opened 2 ♦ , Flan-
   ♥ AQ952     nery. What do you rebid if partner responds
   ♦ 76        each of the following?
   ♣ 94        a) 2 N.T. ___ b) 3♥ ___ c) 4♠ ___
               d) 4♣ ___ e) 2♥ ___ f) 3♣ ___
               g) 3♦ ___

5. ♠ AQ42      Your hand is at left. You opened 2 ♦ , Flan-
   ♥ KQ952     nery. What do you rebid if partner responds
   ♦ K54       each of the following?
   ♣ 9         a) 2 N.T. ___ b) 3♣ ___ c) 4♥ ___
               d) 4♦ ___ e) 2♠ ___ f) 3♣ ___
               g) 3♦ ___

## *Six*

# Forcing No Trump

**Purpose:** To be able to show, with middle-range hands, whether you have 3- or 4-card support for partner's opened major; to find lower suit fits at a low level.

**Natural Bid Given Up:** 1 N.T. response to an opened major, showing 6–9 points and the inability to bid anything else.

**Advantage:** You can show a 2½ raise to partner's major with 3-card support without having to manufacture a suit bid.

If partner opens one of a major, the response of 1 N.T. (ALERTABLE) is forcing and asks opener to describe his hand further. We discuss opener's rebids after looking at the hands with which the responder bids a Forcing No Trump.

The responder bids a Forcing No Trump on hands that have no immediate raise of partner's major, no bid available at the one-level, or not enough points to go to the two-level.

If partner opens one of a major, you respond 1 N.T., and partner rebids two of a lower-ranking suit, the return to two of opener's major shows 2-card support with 5–9 points or 3-card support with 3–5 points.

Partner opens 1 ♠ and you respond 1 N.T. with each of the following hands. Partner then rebids 2 ♣.

| a) | ♠ Q4 | b) | ♠ 985 |
|---|---|---|---|
| | ♥ K765 | | ♥ K542 |
| | ♦ 9764 | | ♦ Q854 |
| | ♣ J52 | | ♣ 94 |
| | Rebid 2 ♠ | | Rebid 2 ♠ |

If partner opens one of a major, you respond 1 N.T., and partner rebids two of a lower-ranking suit, the rebid of 2 N.T. shows two cards in partner's major and 10–12 points with stoppers in the unbid suits. This bid is invitational.

Partner opens 1 ♥ and you respond 1 N.T. Partner rebids 2 ♣ and you hold:

| ♠ KJ3 |
|---|
| ♥ 97 |
| ♦ KJ943 |
| ♣ K93 |
| Rebid 2 N.T. |

If partner opens one of a major, you respond 1 N.T., and partner rebids two of a lower-ranking suit, the rebid of a new suit at the two-level shows a 6-card suit and not enough points to have gone to the two-level immediately.

Partner opens 1 ♥ and you respond 1 N.T. Partner rebids 2 ♣ and you hold:

```
    ♠  K63
    ♥  32
    ♦  KJ9752
    ♣  74

    Rebid 2 ♦
```

If partner opens one of a major, you respond 1 N.T., and partner rebids two of a lower-ranking suit, the jump rebid to three of partner's major shows 10–12 points and 3-card support.

Partner opens 1 ♥ and you respond 1 N.T. Partner rebids 2 ♣ and you hold:

```
    ♠  A5
    ♥  K86
    ♦  K764
    ♣  8532

    Rebid 3 ♥
```

If partner opens one of a major, you respond 1 N.T., and partner rebids two of a lower-ranking suit, pass shows a weak hand and that suit.

Partner opens 1 ♥ and you respond 1 N.T. Partner rebids 2 ♣ and you hold:

```
    ♠  K53
    ♥  9
    ♦  Q986
    ♣  Q7532

    Pass
```

After opening one of a major, if partner responds 1 N.T., you tend to make your normal rebid. A rebid of your opened suit always shows six cards. If you have a lower-ranking 4-card suit, you certainly bid that. With no 6-card major or lower-ranking 4-card suit, you are forced to rebid a 3-card minor. Holding three cards in each minor, rebid clubs. Prefer to rebid a good 6-card major rather than a 4-card minor. With a bad 6-card major, elect to rebid the 4-card minor.

With each of the following hands, partner responds 1 N.T. to your opening bid of 1 ♥.

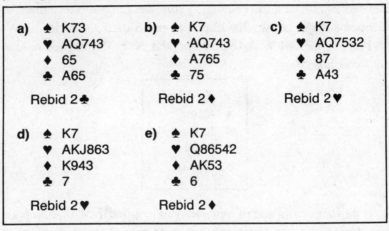

a) ♠ K73
   ♥ AQ743
   ♦ 65
   ♣ A65

   Rebid 2♣

b) ♠ K7
   ♥ AQ743
   ♦ A765
   ♣ 75

   Rebid 2♦

c) ♠ K7
   ♥ AQ7532
   ♦ 87
   ♣ A43

   Rebid 2♥

d) ♠ K7
   ♥ AKJ863
   ♦ K943
   ♣ 7

   Rebid 2♥

e) ♠ K7
   ♥ Q86542
   ♦ AK53
   ♣ 6

   Rebid 2♦

The response of 1 N.T. to a third- or fourth-seat opening bid of a major *tends* to be forcing, but on occasion can be passed. Since a passed hand has many more limited bids available, the opener can pass 1 N.T. with no good rebid.

Most pairs who play the Forcing No Trump also play Limit Raises (see page 74) to show middle-range hands with 4-card support for opener's major.

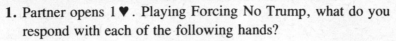

## QUIZ #6

1. Partner opens 1 ♥. Playing Forcing No Trump, what do you respond with each of the following hands?

a)  ♠ A9
    ♥ K73
    ♦ A963
    ♣ 9642 ___

b)  ♠ K84
    ♥ K753
    ♦ J6
    ♣ 8642 ___

c)  ♠ K62
    ♥ Q974
    ♦ A964
    ♣ 102 ___

d)  ♠ K104
    ♥ 75
    ♦ Q864
    ♣ Q1072 ___

e)  ♠ 84
    ♥ 95
    ♦ AQ9752
    ♣ 643 ___

f)  ♠ K73
    ♥ 986
    ♦ Q963
    ♣ 642 ___

g)  ♠ A98
    ♥ 75
    ♦ K743
    ♣ A962 ___

h)  ♠ 963
    ♥ A3
    ♦ K754
    ♣ 8643 ___

2. With each of the following hands you open 1 ♠. What do you rebid if partner responds a Forcing No Trump?

a)  ♠ AK954
    ♥ A74
    ♦ Q84
    ♣ 92 ___

b)  ♠ QJ753
    ♥ KQ92
    ♦ A9
    ♠ 108 ___

c)  ♠ KQJ1064
    ♥ A5
    ♦ 32
    ♣ K65 ___

d)  ♠ AQ532
    ♥ KJ
    ♦ 65
    ♣ K954 ___

e)  ♠ AKQ964
    ♥ 43
    ♦ 5
    ♣ A743 ___

f)  ♠ J97543
    ♥ K4
    ♦ AKJ5
    ♣ 8 ___

# Seven

# Gambling 3 No Trump

**Purpose:** To show a long solid minor suit with little or no outside strength.

**Natural Bid Given Up:** The opening of 3 N.T. to show a balanced hand with 25–27 high-card points.

**Advantage:** To show a specific hand to partner with the hope that he has enough outside strength to bring home a no trump game. This bid also has a preemptive quality, making it difficult for the opponents to exchange information. It may also suggest a sacrifice to partner if the opponents bid on to a major-suit game.

The opening bid of 3 N.T. (ALERTABLE), in first or second position, shows a *solid* 7-card minor suit. Most partnerships agree that it denies an ace or king on the outside. If you do have an ace or king on the outside, it is probably better to open one of your minor. In third position, however, you may have a better hand with honors outside of your suit. Once partner is a passed hand, a slam is unlikely.

You are in first position and hold the following hand:

```
♠  54
♥  32
♦  AKQJ765
♣  Q9
```

Playing Gambling 3 No Trump, you open 3 N.T.

Holding the standard strong 3 N.T. opening bid, you open 2 ♣ and rebid 3 N.T. This shows 25–27 high-card points, balanced.

If partner opens a Gambling 3 No Trump, pass with stoppers in the major suits and keep your fingers crossed.

The response of 4 ♣ (ALERTABLE) to a Gambling 3 No Trump opening bid shows extreme weakness with no chance of making 3 N.T. and asks the opener to pass if his suit is clubs or to bid 4 ♦ if his suit is diamonds.

Partner opens 3 N.T. and you hold the following hand:

```
♠  Q4
♥  Q653
♦  943
♣  7654

Respond 4♣
```

The response of 4 ♦ (ALERTABLE) is forcing and asks opener to rebid a singleton or a void. With a major-suit singleton or void, the opener rebids that major. The rebid of 4 N.T. shows a singleton or void in a minor. If the responder now bids 5 ♣, he wants opener to pass or bid 5 ♦, depending on his long suit. Opener has shown the wrong singleton or void and the responder is no longer interested in slam. With no singleton or void, the opener rebids his suit.

Partner opens 3 N.T. and you hold the following hand:

♠ A8732
♥ 7
♦ AKQ3
♣ 754

Respond 4 ♦

If opener rebids 4 ♥, rebid 5 ♣, which partner will obviously pass. You are likely to have a heart and a spade loser.

If the opener rebids 4 ♠ or 4 N.T., rebid 6 ♣. If partner has a singleton spade, you can take 12 tricks via seven clubs, one spade, three diamonds, and a heart ruff in your hand. If partner has a singleton diamond you can take 12 tricks via seven clubs, discarding two losers on the king and queen of diamonds, the spade ace and a heart ruff in your hand.

The responses of 4 ♥ or 4 ♠ are to play with a self-sufficient 6-card suit or better.

Partner opens 3 N.T. and you hold the following hand:

♠ AKQ987
♥ KQ4
♦ 43
♣ 93

Respond 4 ♠

The response of 5 ♣ shows the desire to play in five of opener's minor suit. This could show a good hand planning to make game, or a preemptive hand taking a save against the opponents' major-suit game.

Partner opens 3 N.T. and you hold each of the following hands:

```
a)   ♠ AK3        b)   ♠ Q4
     ♥ 64              ♥ K65
     ♦ AK763          ♦ 9753
     ♣ 976            ♣ 8743

     Bid 5♣           Bid 5♣
```

The response of 5 ♦ is natural, implying that responder has a club honor and therefore knows the opener's suit is diamonds.

Partner opens 3 N.T. and you hold the following hand:

```
     ♠ A43
     ♥ 42
     ♦ 9865
     ♣ AKQ2

     Bid 5♦
```

The response of 6 ♣ shows the desire to play a minor-suit slam.

Partner opens 3 N.T. and you hold the following hand:

```
     ♠ AK65
     ♥ AK432
     ♦ K
     ♣ 864

     Bid 6♣
```

**Basic Defense:**   A double shows a good hand and is primarily for take-out. If the opponents buy the contract in 3 N.T., it is a good idea to lead an ace. You will get to see dummy, and partner can signal for a continuation or a shift. By not cashing your top tricks, you will often allow a foolish contract to be made.

## *QUIZ # 7*

**1.** Playing Gambling 3 No Trump, what do you open with each of the following hands?

| | | | |
|---|---|---|---|
| **a)** | ♠ 87<br>♥ Q32<br>♦ AKQ7653<br>♣ 6 ___ | **b)** | ♠ K4<br>♥ 643<br>♦ 7<br>♣ AKQ8764 ___ |
| **c)** | ♠ Q53<br>♥ Q8<br>♦ AKJ8642<br>♣ 9 ___ | **d)** | ♠ 72<br>♥ 976<br>♦ 5<br>♣ AKJ9753 ___ |

**2.** Partner opens 3 N.T., Gambling. What do you respond with each of the following hands?

| | | | | | |
|---|---|---|---|---|---|
| **a)** ♠ KQ7<br>♥ A754<br>♦ 864<br>♣ Q63 ___ | | **b)** ♠ KQJ10<br>♥ A74<br>♦ 952<br>♣ AK9 ___ | | **c)** ♠ Q4<br>♥ 987<br>♦ J876<br>♣ 6432 ___ | |
| **d)** ♠ A4<br>♥ AQJ1076<br>♦ Q32<br>♣ 54 ___ | | **e)** ♠ K432<br>♥ K63<br>♦ Q6<br>♣ 9876 ___ | | **f)** ♠ A97654<br>♥ A3<br>♦ 987<br>♣ A3 ___ | |
| **g)** ♠ AK84<br>♥ AK52<br>♦ K<br>♣ 8753 ___ | | | | | |

# *Eight*

# Grand Slam Force

**Purpose:**   To find out whether the partnership has the top three honors in an agreed-upon trump suit.

**Natural Bid Given Up:**   None.

**Advantage:**   To be able to bid a grand slam knowing that you do not have a trump loser.

*After an agreement of suit,* the bid of 5 N.T. is the Grand Slam Force and asks the responder to bid seven of the agreed-upon suit if he holds two of the top three honors. This assumes that the bid cannot be natural or part of another convention (Blackwood, for example). *Without an agreed-upon suit,* the jump to 5 N.T. is the Grand Slam Force, fixing the last bid suit as the agreed-upon suit.

   You open 1 ♦, partner responds 1 ♥, and you rebid 1 ♠. If partner now rebids 5 N.T., spades is the agreed-upon suit.

   Sometimes it's important to know whether the responder to the Grand Slam Force has *one* of the top honors. With this information, the decision may be made to play in no trump instead of the agreed-upon suit.

As long as clubs is not the agreed-upon suit, one or more step responses are available for this purpose.

If diamonds is the agreed-upon suit, the response of 6♦ denies a top honor. The bid of 6♣ shows one of the top honors. Of course, holding two of the top honors the response is 7♦.

If a major is the agreed-upon suit, there are many variations on these step responses. My partner and I have found the Roman Step Responses quite successful.

If the agreed-upon suit is hearts:

1. 6♣ shows none or the queen at best.
2. 6♦ shows four cards to the ace or king.
3. 6♥ shows five cards to the ace or king.
4. 7♥ of course, shows two of the top three honors.

If the agreed-upon suit is spades:

1. 6♣ shows none.
2. 6♦ shows the queen.
3. 6♥ shows four cards to the ace or king.
4. 6♠ shows five to the ace.
5. 7♠ shows two of the top three honors.

Being able to show length and one of the top honors allows the grand slam to be bid with 10-card fits headed by the ace and king.

*Be sure when using the Grand Slam Force that you have one of the top three honors, since partner will bid a grand slam with only two top honors!*

Once a major suit or diamonds is agreed upon and Blackwood has been used, you can no longer use 5 N.T. as the Grand Slam Force since that bid would ask for kings. Therefore, six of an unbid minor, usually clubs, is the Grand Slam Force.

You open 1♠, partner responds 3♠, and you rebid 4 N.T. (Blackwood). Partner rebid 5♥. If you now rebid 6♣, that is the Grand Slam Force.

## *QUIZ #8*

**1.** Partner opens 1 ♠ and with each of the following hands you respond 3 ♠ (forcing). Partner rebids 5 N.T. Grand Slam Force. Playing Roman Step Responses, what do you rebid?

**a)**  ♠ Q865
    ♥ A7
    ♦ A93
    ♣ K943 ___

**b)**  ♠ 9754
    ♥ AKQ
    ♦ A842
    ♣ 97 ___

**c)**  ♠ A8642
    ♥ K7
    ♦ KQ10
    ♣ 1064 ___

**d)**  ♠ K974
    ♥ 73
    ♦ AK9
    ♣ A742 ___

**e)**  ♠ AQ75
    ♥ K8
    ♦ A753
    ♣ 952 ___

# Nine

# Jacoby Transfers

**Purpose:** To allow the opening no trump bidder to play major-suit contracts when the responder has a 5-card or longer major suit.

**Natural Bid Given Up:** When adopting Jacoby, you give up three natural bids. The responses of 2 ♦, 2 ♥, and 2 ♠ to an opening bid of 1 N.T. are no longer to play. However, you do get two of them back (see asterisks * that follow).

**Advantage:** It is usually better to have the lead come up to the stronger hand (the no trump opener) and to have the weaker hand exposed as dummy. Jacoby enables these two conditions to occur.

Playing Jacoby, the response of 2 ♦ (ALERTABLE) to partner's opening bid of 1 N.T. is artificial. This response demands that the opener rebid 2 ♥. The responder guarantees at least a 5-card heart suit and at the moment an unspecified point count. *If the responder has a bad hand and would have bid 2 ♥ to play, *not* playing Jacoby, he now passes and the opening no trump bidder will play in a heart partial.

Partner opens 1 N.T. and you hold the following hand:

♠65 ♥Q98643 ♦842 ♣85. Respond 2♦, and when partner rebids 2♥ (perforce), you pass.

With a game-going hand and five hearts, the responder transfers to hearts by bidding 2♦ and then returns to the number of no trump he would have bid had he not used Jacoby. With eight or nine points and a 5-card heart suit, the responder bids 2♦, transferring to hearts, and then rebids 2 N.T., inviting game in either hearts or no trump.

Partner opens 1 N.T. and you hold: ♠K43 ♥AJ743 ♦642 ♣84. Respond 2♦, and when partner rebids 2♥, you rebid 2 N.T.

The opener must now place the final contract. With only two hearts and a minimum, 16 points, opener passes. With a maximum, 17 or 18 points, he bids 3 N.T., accepting game.

With three or more hearts the opener returns to 3♥ with a minimum, 16 points, and bids game in hearts with a maximum, 17 or 18 points.

With each of the following hands, you open 1 N.T. Partner responds 2♦, Jacoby, and you rebid 2♥. Partner then bids 2 N.T.

| a) | | b) | |
|---|---|---|---|
| ♠ | AQ5 | ♠ | AQ5 |
| ♥ | J6 | ♥ | J6 |
| ♦ | KQ62 | ♦ | KQ62 |
| ♣ | A952 | ♣ | AQ52 |
| | Pass | | Bid 3 N.T. |

| c) | | d) | |
|---|---|---|---|
| ♠ | AQ5 | ♠ | AQ5 |
| ♥ | J62 | ♥ | J62 |
| ♦ | KQ62 | ♦ | KQ62 |
| ♣ | A95 | ♣ | AQ5 |
| | Bid 3♥ | | Bid 4♥ |

With eight or nine points and a 6-card heart suit, the responder bids 2 ♦. After opener rebids 2 ♥, the responder raises to 3 ♥, inviting game in hearts.

Partner opens 1 N.T. and you hold: ♠ A3  ♥ QJ7542  ♦ 843 ♣ 86. Respond 2 ♦, and after partner rebids 2 ♥, you raise to 3 ♥. The opener passes with a minimum, 16 points, and accepts game in hearts with a maximum, 17 or 18 points, even with only two hearts.

With 10–14 points and a 5-card heart suit, the responder bids 2 ♦, transferring to hearts, and then rebids 3 N.T., insisting on game in either hearts or no trump.

Partner opens 1 N.T. and you hold: ♠ A85  ♥ KJ743  ♦ Q5 ♣ 942. Respond 2 ♦. After partner bids 2 ♥, you rebid 3 N.T. With only two hearts, the opening no trump bidder passes. With three or more hearts, the opening no trump bidder corrects to 4 ♥.

With 10–14 points and a 6-card heart suit, the responder bids 2 ♦. After partner rebids 2 ♥, responder rebids 4 ♥, placing the final contract. This, of course, shows the values for game and guarantees that the partnership has at least an 8-card fit. This requires at least a 6-card suit, since the opener may have only a doubleton.

Partner opens 1 N.T. and you hold: ♠ A3  ♥ KQ8732  ♦ Q7 ♣ 842. Respond 2 ♦. After partner rebids 2 ♥, you raise to 4 ♥, placing the final contract.

Playing Jacoby, the response of 2 ♥ (ALERTABLE) to partner's opening bid of 1 N.T. is artificial. This response demands that the opener rebid 2 ♠. The responder guarantees at least a 5-card spade suit and again an unspecified point count. * If the responder has a bad hand and would have bid 2 ♠ to play, *not* playing Jacoby, he now passes and the opener will play in a spade partial.

Partner opens 1 N.T. and you hold: ♠ 986432  ♥ 87  ♦ 843  ♣ 63.

Respond 2♥, and when partner rebids 2♠, you pass. (Don't be surprised if the opponents now enter the auction since you have no points at all.)

With a game-going hand and five spades, the responder transfers to spades by bidding 2♥, and then returns to the number of no trump he would have bid had he not used Jacoby. With eight or nine points and a 5-card spade suit, the responder bids 2♥, transferring to spades and then rebids 2 N.T., inviting game in either spades or no trump.

Partner opens 1 N.T. and you hold: ♠KQ752 ♥74 ♦K432 ♣42. Respond 2♥, and when partner rebids 2♠, you rebid 2 N.T.

Again the opener must place the final contract. With only two spades and 16 points he passes; with 17 or 18 points, he bids 3 N.T. With three or more spades, the opener bids 3♠ with 16 points, and bids game in spades with 17 or 18 points.

With each of the following hands, you open 1 N.T. Partner responds 2♥ and you rebid 2♠. Partner then bids 2 N.T.

| a) | ♠ K643 | b) | ♠ Q2 |
|---|---|---|---|
|  | ♥ 543 |  | ♥ KQ6 |
|  | ♦ AQ7 |  | ♦ KJ63 |
|  | ♣ AQJ |  | ♣ AQ32 |
|  | Bid 3♠ |  | Bid 3 N.T. |
| c) | ♠ 974 | d) | ♠ A2 |
|  | ♥ A4 |  | ♥ KJ76 |
|  | ♦ AK32 |  | ♦ KJ92 |
|  | ♣ AK95 |  | ♣ A42 |
|  | Bid 4♠ |  | Pass |

With eight or nine points and a 6-card spade suit, the responder bids 2♥. After opener rebids 2♠, the responder raises to 3♠, inviting game in spades.

Partner opens 1 N.T. and you hold: ♠KJ7642 ♥72 ♦Q65 ♣J3. Respond 2♥, and after partner rebids 2♠, raise to 3♠. The opener passes with a minimum, 16 points, and accepts game in spades with a maximum, 17 or 18 points, even with only two spades.

With 10–14 points and a 5-card spade suit, the responder bids 2♥, transferring to spades, and then rebids 3 N.T., the number of no trump he would have bid had he not used Jacoby. This insists on game in either spades or no trump.

Partner opens 1 N.T. and you hold: ♠AQ764 ♥Q32 ♦K54 ♣102. Respond 2♥, and after partner bids 2♠, you rebid 3 N.T. With only two spades the opener passes. With three or more spades the opener corrects to 4♠.

With 10–14 points and a 6-card spade suit, the responder bids 2♥, and, after partner rebids 2♠, responder rebids 4♠, placing the final contract. This shows the values for game and guarantees a 6-card suit, assuring that the partnership has at least an 8-card fit.

Partner opens 1 N.T. and you hold: ♠KQJ876 ♥3 ♦K4 ♣8743. Respond 2♥, and after partner rebids 2♠, you bid 4♠, placing the final contract.

Holding both a 5- and a 4-card major, the responder should not transfer. Use Stayman and if partner rebids either major, invite game in that major with eight or nine points, and bid game in that major with 10–14 points. If the opener rebids 2♦, you may now bid your 5-card major at the two-level with eight or nine points, and at the three-level with 10–14 points.

Partner opens 1 N.T. and you hold: ♠KJ743 ♥A543 ♦75 ♣92. Respond 2♣. If partner rebids 2♥ or 2♠, rebid 4♥ or 4♠, respectively. However, if partner rebids 2♦, you should rebid 2♠.

Holding two 5-card majors, you should transfer to spades and then bid the appropriate number of hearts. With eight or nine points, including distribution, rebid 3 ♥. This invites game in either major, asking opener to pay particular attention to his major-suit holding and probably requiring aces in the minors. With 10–14 points, rebid 4 ♥, asking partner to take his choice of major-suit games.

Partner opens 1 N.T. and with each of the following hands you bid 2 ♥, transferring to 2 ♠.

| a) | ♠ KJ763 | b) | ♠ AQ864 |
|----|---------|----|---------|
|    | ♥ QJ942 |    | ♥ KJ932 |
|    | ♦ 8     |    | ♦ 8     |
|    | ♣ 53    |    | ♣ 53    |
|    | Rebid 3 ♥ |  | Rebid 4 ♥ |

If the responder transfers to a major suit and then rebids a minor suit, he is showing a two-suited hand. The rebid of a minor at the three-level is forcing and it is now up to the opener to make the next move. If he rebids 3 N.T., he is not interested in responder's major (having only two cards in the suit) or slam in the minor. If he bids one of the other two suits, he shows the ace of that suit and interest in slam in one of responder's suits, which is likely to be clarified by his next bid.

Since we no longer use 2 ♠ to play, this response is assigned a new meaning. I like to call it minor-suit Stayman. The bid of 2 ♠ (ALERTABLE) asks the opening no trump bidder whether he has a 4-card minor. The responder must have at least four cards in each minor. (This bid should be reserved for hands with minor-suit slam interest, that is, 15-plus points; otherwise, simply bid the appropriate number of no trump.) The opener rebids a 4-card minor suit; if he has none he rebids 2 N.T. If the opener rebids 2 N.T., responder's rebid of 3 ♠ (ALERTABLE) asks the opener to bid a 3-card minor, guarantees 5–5 in the minors, and shows continued interest in slam. This is very useful, since we all know that it is often difficult to bid minor-suit slams.

With the adoption of Jacoby, many pairs now play that the direct jump to 3 ♣ or 3 ♦ (ALERTABLE) after partner opens 1 N.T. is preemptive. The direct jumps to 3 ♥ or 3 ♠ are still slam-oriented in the respective suit. The response of 2 ♣ to partner's 1 N.T. opening, followed by the bid of a minor (ALERTABLE), shows slam interest in that minor.

For example: 1 N.T.—2 ♣—2 ♥—3 ♣, slam interest in clubs; 1 N.T.—2 ♣—2 ♥—3 ♦, slam interest in diamonds.

Jacoby is "off" if the opponents bid over partner's opening bid of 1 N.T.

It is generally accepted not to use Jacoby after 1 N.T. overcalls, when it is usually more important to be able to bid two of any suit to play.

If partner opens 2 N.T., 3 ♦ (ALERTABLE) is a transfer to 3 ♥, and 3 ♥ (ALERTABLE) is a transfer to 3 ♠. The responder may pass, not wishing to play game, or bid 4 ♥ or 4 ♠ with a 6-card suit and values for game, or bid 3 N.T. with a 5-card major and the values for game. 3 ♠ (ALERTABLE ) asks for the minors and shows interest in slam.

**Basic Defense:** If left-hand opponent opens 1 N.T., partner passes, and right-hand opponent transfers, 2 N.T. shows the minors. Double (ALERTABLE) shows the transfer suit and the other nontouching suit. (Double of hearts shows hearts and clubs; double of diamonds shows diamonds and spades.) A cue bid in the responder's real suit (ALERTABLE) shows the other two suits of the same color. (If responder bids 2 ♦, the bid of 2 ♥ shows clubs and spades. If the responder bids 2 ♥, the bid of 2 ♠ shows diamonds and hearts.)

## QUIZ #9

1. Partner opens 1 N.T. Playing Jacoby, what do you respond with each of the following hands? If partner's rebid is forced, also designate your planned rebid.

a) ♠ KJ743
♥ QJ5
♦ J3
♣ 963 ___

b) ♠ 76
♥ KJ7654
♦ 75
♣ 1098 ___

c) ♠ KQ8632
♥ A3
♦ 9865
♣ 6 ___

d) ♠ 54
♥ KQ9875
♦ Q54
♣ 42 ___

e) ♠ AQ853
♥ A65
♦ 85
♣ 432 ___

f) ♠ J109753
♥ 74
♦ 432
♣ 96 ___

g) ♠ K2
♥ AJ1076
♦ K53
♣ 963 ___

h) ♠ KQ754
♥ AJ54
♦ 76
♣ 107 ___

i) ♠ A2
♥ KJ7642
♦ 43
♣ Q53 ___

j) ♠ K98643
♥ K42
♦ 864
♣ 9 ___

k) ♠ 3
♥ K32
♦ KQ84
♣ AK652 ___

l) ♠ KJ953
♥ QJ752
♦ 9
♣ 73 ___

m) ♠ KJ765
♥ 5
♦ A3
♣ KQJ75 ___

n) ♠ 543
♥ KQJ65
♦ 74
♣ Q92 ___

o) ♠ QJ854
♥ AK642
♦ 5
♣ 106 ___

**2.**   ♠ K4       Your hand is at left and you open 1 N.T.

     ♥ QJ5        a) Partner responds 2 ♥ and you rebid 2 ♠.

     ♦ A543     What do you rebid if partner now rebids

     ♣ AQ82    2 N.T._____? 3 N.T._____?

                   b) Partner responds 2 ♦ and you rebid 2 ♥.
                   What do you rebid if partner now rebids
                   2 N.T._____? 3 N.T._____?

**3.**   ♠ A63      Your hand is at left and you open 1 N.T.

     ♥ K5         a) Partner responds 2 ♥ and you rebid 2 ♠.

     ♦ KQ62    What do you rebid if partner now rebids

     ♣ AQ97    2 N.T._____? 3 N.T._____? 3 ♠ _____?

                   b) Partner responds 2 ♦ and you rebid 2 ♥.
                   What do you rebid if partner now rebids
                   2 N.T._____? 3 N.T._____? 3 ♥ _____?

# *Ten*

# Jacoby 2 No Trump

**Purpose:** To show a strong major-suit raise, usually when playing limit raises or most assuredly when playing Forcing No Trump.

**Natural Bid Given Up:** The response of 2 N.T. to a major-suit opening to show a balanced hand and 13–15 points.

**Advantage:** By using the 2 N.T. bid as a forcing raise, you leave more room for opener to describe his hand further.

Playing Jacoby 2 No Trump, if partner opens one of a major, the response of 2 N.T. (ALERTABLE) shows an opening bid and 4-card support for partner's major.

Playing Jacoby 2 No Trump, partner opens 1 ♠ and you hold the following hand:

> ♠ K876
> ♥ 76
> ♦ AQ76
> ♣ A75
>
> Respond 2 N.T.

If the responder bids 2 N.T., Jacoby, after a major suit opening, the opener has five basic rebids.

The rebid of a new suit at the three-level (ALERTABLE) shows a singleton or a void in that suit.

You open 1 ♥ and partner responds 2 N.T., Jacoby. You hold the following hand:

---

♠ 6
♥ AQ765
♦ A43
♣ K643

Rebid 3 ♠,
showing your
singleton

---

The rebid of a new suit at the four-level (ALERTABLE) shows a 5-card suit. You, of course, must have a singleton or a void in one of the unbid suits, since you are now showing a 5-5 hand.

You open 1 ♥ and partner responds 2 N.T., Jacoby. You hold the following hand:

---

♠ A3
♥ KQ876
♦ KJ765
♣ 5

Rebid 4 ♦,
showing a
5-card suit

---

The rebid of four of the opened major (ALERTABLE) shows a minimum flat hand with no interest in slam.

You open 1 ♥ and partner responds 2 N.T., Jacoby. You hold the following hand:

```
♠ K43
♥ AKJ76
♦ Q43
♣ 94

Rebid 4 ♥ to
show no interest
in going further
```

The rebid of three of the opened major (ALERTABLE) shows a good hand, forward going, and tends to show a 6-card suit.

You open 1 ♥ and partner responds 2 N.T., Jacoby. You hold the following hand:

```
♠ A5
♥ AQ8753
♦ KJ6
♣ 43

Rebid 3 ♥,
showing some
interest in slam
```

The rebid of 3 N.T. shows a balanced hand with a little extra, and values outside of the opened suit.

You open 1 ♥ and partner responds 2 N.T., Jacoby. You hold the following hand:

```
♠ K7
♥ K7653
♦ AJ6
♣ KJ2

Rebid 3 N.T.
```

## *QUIZ #10*

1. Partner opens 1 ♠. Playing Jacoby, what do you respond with each of the following hands?

a)
♠ K76
♥ A3
♦ KQ76
♣ J765 ___

b)
♠ QJ87
♥ K9
♦ K876
♣ A83 ___

c)
♠ J6
♥ KJ6
♦ QJ65
♣ AQ32 ___

2. With each of the following hands you open 1 ♠. Partner responds 2 N.T., Jacoby. What do you rebid?

a)
♠ KJ765
♥ Q76
♦ A43
♣ K6 ___

b)
♠ AQ986
♥ 5
♦ KJ65
♣ A96 ___

c)
♠ AK8432
♥ K4
♦ A43
♣ 94 ___

d)
♠ AJ1095
♥ KQ765
♦ A2
♣ 4 ___

e)
♠ 97543
♥ KJ6
♦ AQ
♣ A87 ___

# *Eleven*

# Jordan

**Purpose:**   To be able to make a limit raise after partner opens the bidding and right-hand opponent makes a take-out double.

**Natural Bid Given Up:**   None.

**Advantage:**   To be able to bid the full value of your hand, showing support for partner's opened suit without having to redouble first.

If partner opens the bidding and right-hand opponent doubles, the response of 2 N.T. (ALERTABLE) is artificial. This is Jordan, showing a hand worth 9–11 points and at least 4-card support in partner's opened suit.

Partner opens 1 ♥, right-hand opponent doubles, and you hold: ♠ 864  ♥ QJ94  ♦ KQ43  ♣ Q6. Playing Jordan, you respond 2 N.T., showing the full value of your hand with one bid. If the opener is minimum and does not wish to go on to game, he rebids his opened suit at the three-level (in this example, 3 ♥). This makes it very difficult for the opponents to compete. Using standard methods with this example, you would have to redouble, showing 10 or more points, of course planning to raise hearts at your next opportunity. However, left-hand opponent may bid 1 ♠ over your redouble; partner is likely to pass, as requested; and right-hand opponent may now really sock it to you by bidding 3 ♠. Should you double, bid 4 ♥, or pass? I don't know, either. If you had used Jordan, this dilemma probably would not have occurred. It is unlikely that left-hand opponent would have bid over 2 N.T., and if partner rebids 3 ♥, showing a minimum hand, you probably would have bought the contract. Therefore, Jordan has a preemptive quality as well.

If a major suit is opened and the responder uses Jordan, the opener's rebid of four of that major naturally shows extra values for game. A new suit by the opener is a cue bid and suggests the possibility of a slam. The responder should cue bid an ace if he has one. Not having an ace, the responder simply returns to the agreed-upon major.

With each of the following hands, you open 1 ♥ and partner responds 2 N.T., Jordan, after left-hand opponent doubles. Right-hand opponent passes.

| a) | ♠ | 76 | b) | ♠ | 9 | c) | ♠ | 76 |
|----|---|-----|----|---|--------|----|---|--------|
|    | ♥ | AQ754 |    | ♥ | AQ7543 |    | ♥ | AQ864 |
|    | ♦ | KJ6 |    | ♦ | K2 |    | ♦ | KQ2 |
|    | ♣ | K65 |    | ♣ | AQJ4 |    | ♣ | A64 |
|    | **Rebid 3 ♥** | | | **Rebid 3 ♣** | | | **Rebid 4 ♥** | |

If a minor suit is opened and the responder uses Jordan, the opener's rebid of 3 N.T. is to play, showing extra values for game and stoppers in the unbid suits. Opener's rebid of a new suit at the three-level shows the values for game but not necessarily interest in slam. He may be showing a suit in which he has stoppers, hoping that the responder can now bid 3 N.T.

With each of the following hands, you opened 1♣. Left-hand opponent doubles and partner responds 2 N.T., Jordan.

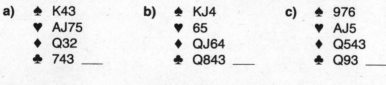

a)  ♠ KJ5          b)  ♠ 865
    ♥ AQ32             ♥ AQ32
    ♦ K82              ♦ K82
    ♣ Q73              ♣ AQ9

    Rebid 3 N.T.       Rebid 3♥


## *QUIZ #11*

1. Partner opens 1 ♥. Playing Jordan, what do you respond with each of the following hands after right-hand opponent doubles?

a)  ♠ K43          b)  ♠ KJ4          c)  ♠ 976
    ♥ AJ75             ♥ 65               ♥ AJ5
    ♦ Q32              ♦ QJ64             ♦ Q543
    ♣ 743 ___          ♣ Q843 ___         ♣ Q93 ___

d)  ♠ 83           e)  ♠ 76
    ♥ AJ432            ♥ AJ3
    ♦ 43               ♦ K432
    ♣ Q743 ___         ♣ Q532 ___

**2.** Partner opens 1 ♦ . Playing Jordan, what do you respond with each of the following hands after right-hand opponent doubles?

**a)** ♠ 863
♥ KQ64
♦ KJ32
♣ 42 ___

**b)** ♠ 76
♥ AQ3
♦ KJ43
♣ 9652 ___

**c)** ♠ 95
♥ A54
♦ K7643
♣ 865 ___

**d)** ♠ K3
♥ 76
♦ QJ9862
♣ 643 ___

**e)** ♠ 763
♥ AQ75
♦ A76
♣ 975 ___

**f)** ♠ QJ10
♥ KJ3
♦ 9765
♣ Q109 ___

# *Twelve*

# Landy

**Purpose:** To be able to show major suits after an opponent's opening bid of 1 N.T.

**Natural Bid Given Up:** The bid of 2♣ to show clubs after an opponent opens 1 N.T.

**Advantage:** To be able to compete with a two-suited major-suit hand without extreme distribution.

The overcall of 2♣ (ALERTABLE) after an opponent's bid of 1 N.T. shows at least four cards in each major. If you have only four cards in each major, you should have at least an opening bid. As your suits get longer, you may have fewer points. You again can take greater liberties with favorable vulnerability.

Right-hand opponent opens 1 N.T. and you hold each of the following hands:

| a) | ♠ KQ76 | b) | ♠ QJ1097 | c) | ♠ K874 |
|----|---------|-----|-----------|-----|---------|
|    | ♥ AQ76  |     | ♥ AQ876   |     | ♥ QJ87  |
|    | ♦ A2    |     | ♦ 4       |     | ♦ K65   |
|    | ♣ 854   |     | ♣ QJ      |     | ♣ Q4    |
|    | Bid 2♣  |     | Bid 2♣    |     | Pass    |

Landy may be used over a weak or strong no trump, in the direct or balancing seat, depending on partnership agreement.

The overcalls of 2♦, 2♥, and 2♠ are still natural, showing one-suited hands. You must overcall 3♣ to show a one-suited club hand.

The following are suggested responses to Landy. Bid 2♥ or 2♠ to play with no interest in game.

Partner overcalls 2♣ after left-hand opponent opens 1 N.T. Right-hand opponent passes and you hold the following hands:

| a) | ♠ K543 | b) | ♠ A2 |
|----|---------|-----|-------|
|    | ♥ 86    |     | ♥ 975 |
|    | ♦ Q854  |     | ♦ J875 |
|    | ♣ 853   |     | ♣ Q1062 |
|    | Bid 2♠  |     | Bid 2♥ |

The responses of 3♥ or 3♠ are invitations to game and may be made on a 3-card suit. The Landy bidder is rarely 4–4, more often 5–4 or 5–5.

Partner overcalls 2♣, Landy, after left-hand opponent opens 1 N.T. Right-hand opponent passes and you hold the following hands:

```
a)  ♠ KJ65      b)  ♠ 9
    ♥ Q3            ♥ A987
    ♦ AQ65          ♦ 765
    ♣ 754           ♣ AQ876

    Bid 3 ♠         Bid 3 ♥
```

The responses of 4 ♥ or 4 ♠ are naturally to play and show hands with which you think you can make game.

Partner overcalls 2 ♣, Landy, after left-hand opponent opens 1 N.T. Right-hand opponent passes and you hold the following hands:

```
a)  ♠ AQ76      b)  ♠ J109
    ♥ A3            ♥ AK765
    ♦ KJ7653        ♦ 43
    ♣ 5             ♣ AQ3

    Bid 4 ♠         Bid 4 ♥
```

3 ♣ (ALERTABLE) is the only forcing response and asks the Landy bidder to pick his longer major. The responder has equal length in the majors and is suggesting game.

Left-hand opponent opens 1 N.T. and partner overcalls 2 ♣, Landy. Right-hand opponent passes. You hold the following hand: ♠ KJ76 ♥ AJ64 ♦ Q9 ♣ 754. Bid 3 ♣. The Landy bidder may rebid 3 ♥ or 3 ♠ with a minimum take-out and no interest in game.

Partner responds 3 ♣ to your Landy take-out and you hold each of the following hands:

a) ♠ AQ32      b) ♠ A9764
   ♥ K10963      ♥ KQ64
   ♦ 75          ♦ 9
   ♣ 64          ♣ 973

   Bid 3 ♥        Bid 3 ♠

Of course, you bid Landy on these hands with favorable vulnerability.

If partner bids 3 ♣ in response to your Landy bid, you should bid 4 ♥ or 4 ♠ with a maximum, accepting game.

Partner responds 3 ♣ to your Landy take-out and you hold each of the following hands:

a) ♠ AQ843    b) ♠ A964
   ♥ K742      ♥ KQ1032
   ♦ 9          ♦ A73
   ♣ A72       ♣ 9

   Bid 4 ♠        Bid 4 ♥

2 N.T. and 3 ♦ in response to partner's Landy take-out are natural. Both bids show good hands and are invitational, but not forcing.

Left-hand opponent opens 1 N.T., partner bids 2 ♣, Landy, and right-hand opponent passes. You hold each of the following hands:

a) ♠ 94        b) ♠ Q3
   ♥ Q74       ♥ Q3
   ♦ KJ53     ♦ KQJ753
   ♣ AJ73     ♣ J63

   Bid 2 N.T.     Bid 3 ♦

The response of 2 ♦ to the Landy bidder shows a weak hand with long diamonds.

Left-hand opponent opens 1 N.T. Partner bids 2 ♣, Landy, and right-hand opponent passes. You hold the following hand: ♠ 82 ♥ 73 ♦ KJ86432 ♣ Q8. Bid 2 ♦.

A pass in response to Landy shows a weak hand with long clubs.

Again left-hand opponent opens 1 N.T. and partner bids 2 ♣, Landy. Right-hand opponent passes. You hold the following hand: ♠ 76 ♥ Q2 ♦ Q72 ♣ KJ10984. Pass.

**Basic Defense:** Double of the Landy 2 ♣ bid may be used in two ways, again depending on partnership agreement. It may be used to show clubs, or it may be used to show a good hand with defense against the majors, to suggest defending. 2 N.T. can be natural, showing a hand that you would have bid 2 N.T. without the Landy bid. It may also be used as unusual, asking the opening no trump bidder to bid a minor suit. If you adopt this meaning, you should double and then bid 2 N.T. with the hand with which you would have responded 2 N.T. without the Landy bid.

## *QUIZ #12*

---

**1.** Right-hand opponent opens 1 N.T. Playing Landy, what do you bid with each of the following hands? Assume favorable vulnerability.

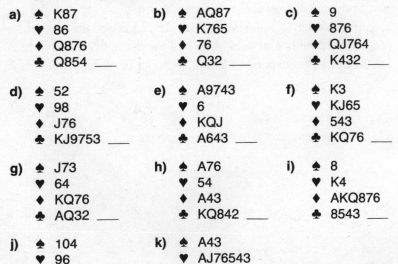

**a)** ♠ KJ854
♥ QJ1076
♦ Q3
♣ 4 ___

**b)** ♠ AQ97
♥ KQJ7
♦ K3
♣ 942 ___

**c)** ♠ J9765
♥ QJ765
♦ 5
♣ 95 ___

**d)** ♠ AQJ765
♥ 87
♦ A43
♣ Q3 ___

**e)** ♠ A2
♥ 43
♦ 754
♣ AKJ1098 ___

**2.** Left-hand opponent opens 1 N.T. Partner overcalls 2♣, Landy. What do you bid with each of the following hands if right-hand opponent passes?

**a)** ♠ K87
♥ 86
♦ Q876
♣ Q854 ___

**b)** ♠ AQ87
♥ K765
♦ 76
♣ Q32 ___

**c)** ♠ 9
♥ 876
♦ QJ764
♣ K432 ___

**d)** ♠ 52
♥ 98
♦ J76
♣ KJ9753 ___

**e)** ♠ A9743
♥ 6
♦ KQJ
♣ A643 ___

**f)** ♠ K3
♥ KJ65
♦ 543
♣ KQ76 ___

**g)** ♠ J73
♥ 64
♦ KQ76
♣ AQ32 ___

**h)** ♠ A76
♥ 54
♦ A43
♣ KQ842 ___

**i)** ♠ 8
♥ K4
♦ AKQ876
♣ 8543 ___

**j)** ♠ 104
♥ 96
♦ KJ108654
♣ 72 ___

**k)** ♠ A43
♥ AJ76543
♦ 6
♣ 65 ___

# *Thirteen*

# Lebensohl Over No Trump

**Purpose:** To enable the responder to a 1 N.T. opening bid to invite game or place the final contract below game, after right-hand opponent overcalls.

**Natural Bid Given Up:** The response of 2 N.T., invitational, after right-hand opponent overcalls partner's opening bid of 1 N.T.

**Advantage:** To be able to get out at the three-level after partner opens 1 N.T. and right-hand opponent overcalls.

If partner opens 1 N.T. and right-hand opponent overcalls at the two-level, the bid of 2 N.T. (ALERTABLE), playing Lebensohl, requires the opener to rebid 3 ♣. If the responder then rebids a suit at the three-level, it is to play.

Partner opens 1 N.T., right-hand opponent overcalls 2 ♠, and you hold the following hand: ♠ 54 ♥ KJ7543 ♦ Q5 ♣ 874. Respond 2 N.T., and when partner rebids 3 ♣, you rebid 3 ♥ to play.

A direct response at the three-level (without a jump) is invitational.

Again partner opens 1 N.T. and right-hand opponent overcalls 2♠. This time you hold: ♠83 ♥KJ8532 ♦54 ♣K53. Respond 3♥, inviting game in hearts.

If partner opens 1 N.T., right-hand opponent overcalls, and you can bid your suit at the two-level, a two-level response is to play. A jump response at the three-level is forcing, and 2 N.T. followed by three of your suit is invitational.

Partner opens 1 N.T. and right-hand opponent overcalls 2♦. You hold each of the following hands:

| a) | | b) | | c) | |
|---|---|---|---|---|---|
| ♠ | 85 | ♠ | 854 | ♠ | 94 |
| ♥ | KJ10754 | ♥ | AQ8754 | ♥ | AQ963 |
| ♦ | 75 | ♦ | 9 | ♦ | KJ7 |
| ♣ | 954 | ♣ | J85 | ♣ | 942 |
| | | | | | |
| Bid 2♥ to play | | Bid 2 N.T. fol-lowed by 3♥ invitational | | Bid 3♥ forcing | |

If partner opens 1 N.T. and right-hand opponent overcalls, the response of 3 N.T. (ALERTABLE) shows at least 10 points, but denies a stopper in the overcalled suit.

Partner opens 1 N.T., right-hand opponent overcalls 2♠, and you hold: ♠86 ♥KJ4 ♦A432 ♣Q854. Respond 3 N.T., denying a spade stopper.

If partner opens 1 N.T. and right-hand opponent overcalls, the response of 2 N.T., relaying to 3♣, followed by 3 N.T. (ALERTABLE) shows at least 10 points and a stopper in the overcalled suit.

Partner opens 1 N.T., right-hand opponent overcalls 2♠, and you hold: ♠A4 ♥KJ5 ♦K854 ♣643. Respond 2 N.T., and after partner rebids 3♣, rebid 3 N.T.

A fast auction denies a stopper, and a slow auction shows a stopper in the opponent's suit.

If partner opens 1 N.T. and right-hand opponent overcalls at the two-level, a cue bid of the overcalled suit (ALERTABLE) is Stayman (standard procedure) with the values for game. However, with the adoption of Lebensohl, this auction denies a stopper in the overcalled suit.

Partner opens 1 N.T., right-hand opponent overcalls 2♠, and you hold the following hand: ♠65 ♥KJ76 ♦543 ♣AQ53. Respond 3♠.

Having a stopper in the overcalled suit, you respond 2 N.T., and after partner rebids 3♣, you then cue bid the overcalled suit (ALERTABLE). Again, this is Stayman, but promises a stopper in the overcalled suit.

Partner opens 1 N.T., right-hand opponent overcalls 2♠, and you hold: ♠A5 ♥KJ76 ♦765 ♣Q854. Respond 2 N.T., and after partner rebids 3♣, you rebid 3♠.

Again, a fast auction denies a stopper, whereas a slow auction shows a stopper.

## *Quiz #13*

---

1. Partner opens 1 N.T. and right-hand opponent overcalls 2 ♥.
   Playing Lebensohl, what do you respond with each of the following hands? If partner's response is forced, what is your
   planned rebid?

**a)**
♠ KJ7654
♥ 54
♦ 876
♣ 43 ___

**b)**
♠ AQ54
♥ 94
♦ KJ65
♣ 953 ___

**c)**
♠ KQ765
♥ 86
♦ K54
♣ 642 ___

**d)**
♠ 87
♥ 97
♦ KJ109765
♣ 95 ___

**e)**
♠ AQJ765
♥ 54
♦ K43
♣ 72 ___

**f)**
♠ A4
♥ 643
♦ 54
♣ KJ7654 ___

**g)**
♠ KQ65
♥ KJ4
♦ 43
♣ Q654 ___

**h)**
♠ AQ5
♥ 96
♦ KJ94
♣ 9742 ___

**i)**
♠ A96
♥ K87
♦ Q987
♣ K92 ___

# *Fourteen*

# Lebensohl Over Weak Two-Bids

**Purpose:** To be able to get out at the three-level after partner doubles an opponent's opening weak two-bid.

**Natural Bid Given Up:** 2 N.T. in response to partner's take-out double of an opponent's opening weak two-bid.

**Advantage:** To be able to bid at the three-level without inviting game and still handle game-going hands.

If partner doubles left-hand opponent's opening weak two-bid and right-hand opponent passes, the bid of 2 N.T. (ALERTABLE) forces partner to rebid 3 ♣. If you have a weak hand with clubs you now pass.

Left-hand opponent opens 2 ♥, weak. Partner doubles and you hold: ♠95 ♥986 ♦Q4 ♣KJ8642. Respond 2 N.T., and when partner rebids 3 ♣, you pass.

Holding a weak hand with a suit other than clubs, you respond 2 N.T., and when partner rebids 3 ♣, perforce, you bid your suit at the three-level to play. The take-out doubler now passes.

Left-hand opponent opens 2 ♠, weak, and partner doubles. Right-hand opponent passes and you hold: ♠43 ♥854 ♦KQ8754 ♣Q3. Respond 2 N.T., and when partner rebids 3 ♣, you rebid 3 ♦, setting the final contract. Of course, partner might go on if he has a super hand.

Direct three-level responses vary depending on the suit opened. Let's look at all possibilities.

Left-hand opponent opens 2 ♠, partner doubles, and right-hand opponent passes.

1. 2 N.T. followed by three of a suit is to play.
2. Any direct three-level response (3 ♣, 3 ♦, or 3 ♥) is invitational.

Left-hand opponent opens 2 ♥, partner doubles, and right-hand opponent passes.

1. 2 ♠ is to play.
2. 2 N.T. followed by 3 ♦ is to play.
3. 2 N.T. followed by pass after partner rebids 3 ♣ is obviously to play.
4. 2 N.T. followed by 3 ♠ is invitational.
5. 3 ♣ or 3 ♦, direct, are invitational.
6. A direct jump to 3 ♠ is forcing.

Left-hand opponent opens 2 ♦, partner doubles, and right-hand opponent passes.

1. 2 ♥ or 2 ♠ is to play.
2. 2 N.T. followed by passing partner's rebid of 3 ♣ is again to play.
3. 2 N.T. followed by 3 ♥ or 3 ♠ is invitational.
4. 3 ♣, direct, is invitational.
5. A direct jump to 3 ♥ or 3 ♠ is forcing.

If left-hand opponent opens a weak two-bid, in any suit, and partner doubles, the response of 3 N.T. is to play, showing a stopper in the opened suit and the values for game. The response of 2 N.T. followed by 3 N.T. shows a double-stopper in the opened suit.

## QUIZ #14

1. Left-hand opponent opens a weak 2 ♦. Partner doubles and right-hand opponent passes. Playing Lebensohl, what do you respond with each of the following hands? Indicate any planned rebid.

a)  ♠ K4
    ♥ 54
    ♦ 865
    ♣ Q97532 ___

b)  ♠ QJ765
    ♥ 65
    ♦ 986
    ♣ J76 ___

c)  ♠ Q6
    ♥ Q4
    ♦ 876
    ♣ KQJ864 ___

d)  ♠ KJ765
    ♥ 65
    ♦ AQ5
    ♣ J75 ___

e)  ♠ 93
    ♥ AQ8754
    ♦ A65
    ♣ Q4 ___

f)  ♠ A76
    ♥ KQ3
    ♦ Q75
    ♣ A762 ___

g)  ♠ J65
    ♥ Q4
    ♦ AJ105
    ♣ AJ32 ___

# *Fifteen*

# Limit Raises

**Purpose:** To enable the responder to show the full value of middle-range hands, 9–11 points, with one bid. This, therefore, often eliminates the need to manufacture a bid.

**Natural Bid Given Up:** The jump response to three of partner's opened suit showing a full opening bid, forcing to game.

**Advantage:** Since most experts agree that the middle-range hands are the most difficult to bid, limit raises afford the ability to show them quickly and efficiently.

The jump raise of opener's suit (from 1 to 3) no longer shows an opening bid, but is now limited to 9–11 points with at least 4-card support. Using limit raises, you can *invite* game with one bid. Limit raises also have a preemptive quality, making it very difficult for the opponents to compete for partials. (The bidding is already at the three-level.)

Partner opens 1 ♥, right-hand opponent passes, and you hold each of the following hands:

| a) | ♠ K4     | b) | ♠ 62    | c) | ♠ QJ5   |
|----|----------|----|---------|----|---------|
|    | ♥ QJ87   |    | ♥ 9863  |    | ♥ K864  |
|    | ♦ K543   |    | ♦ AK32  |    | ♦ J85   |
|    | ♣ 842    |    | ♣ Q75   |    | ♣ Q73   |

| d) | ♠ A854   | e) | ♠ A85   |
|----|----------|----|---------|
|    | ♥ KQ7    |    | ♥ KQ75  |
|    | ♦ 632    |    | ♦ 853   |
|    | ♣ 973    |    | ♣ Q82   |

With hand a), respond 3 ♥.

With hand b), respond 3 ♥. With the doubleton spade, your hand evaluates to 10 points, and with diamond controls, your hand is a little too good to simply raise to 2 ♥.

With hand c), respond only 2 ♥. Remember, a simple raise of partner's suit still shows 6–10 points. With overlap of point count you have to judge the worth of your hand. Since you are so balanced, you should not make a limit raise. If partner can't move over your 2 ♥ bid, there is unlikely to be a game.

With hand d), respond 1 ♠. You must have 4-card support to make a limit raise.

With hand e), respond 3 ♥. Here a limit raise is called for even with a balanced hand, since you have 11 high-card points. This example shows the difficulty in bidding if you have *not* adopted limit raises. This hand has no legitimate bid using standard methods.

The limit raise in a major suit naturally invites game in that major. The opener should accept with a maximum and pass with a minimum opening bid. He may even try for slam with a very strong hand.

The limit raise in a minor suit suggests game possibilities and denies a 4-card major. Holding enough points, the partnership will usually bid game in no trump. Often the opener will simply rebid 3 N.T. If the opener rebids a suit at the three-level, he is maximum, accepting game, and showing values in that suit. He does not have stoppers in all the unbid suits and is hoping you can now bid 3 N.T. If you have stoppers in the unbid suits, you should bid 3 N.T. You may be able to show values in a third suit at the three-level, alllowing partner to bid 3 N.T. with the fourth suit stopped. Study the following example.

|  | NORTH | SOUTH |
|---|---|---|
| ♠ | 8432 | A76 |
| ♥ | AKQ | 753 |
| ♦ | A8 | 74 |
| ♣ | Q642 | AK975 |

| SOUTH | WEST | NORTH | EAST |
|---|---|---|---|
|  |  | 1♣ | Pass |
| 3♣ | Pass | 3♥ | Pass |
| 3♠ | Pass | 3 N.T. | Pass |
| Pass | Pass |  |  |

Since it is important to be able to show a strong raise in partner's opened major (13–16 points with at least 4-card support), a standard procedure playing limit raises is to use a jump to 3 N.T. (ALERTABLE) to show the strong hand. (Also, see Jacoby 2 No Trump.) This bid no longer shows an opening no trump hand with 4-3-3-3 distribution.

Partner opens 1♠, right-hand opponent passes, and you hold: ♠Q874 ♥A4 ♦KJ76 ♣A62. Respond 3 N.T.

With the adoption of the limit raise structure, even secondary jumps by responder are limit and nonforcing. If partner opens 1♦, you respond 1♥, and partner rebids 1♠, the following jumps are limit:

• Jump rebid to 3♦ showing 4-card support and 9–11 points.

• Jump rebid to 3♠ showing normal trump support (four cards) and 9–11 points.

• Jump rebid to 2 N.T. showing stoppers in the unbid suits and 10–12 points.

• Jump rebid to 3♥ shows a 6-card suit and 10–12 points. These bids all invite game but are nonforcing.

Partner opens 1♦, right-hand opponent passes, you respond 1♥, left-hand opponent passes, and partner rebids 1♠. Right-hand opponent again passes and you hold each of the following hands:

| a) | ♠ K7 | b) | ♠ K743 |
|---|---|---|---|
| | ♥ AQ64 | | ♥ Q754 |
| | ♦ Q643 | | ♦ AJ3 |
| | ♣ 874 | | ♣ 73 |
| | Rebid 3♦ | | Rebid 3♠ |
| c) | ♠ 32 | d) | ♠ Q8 |
| | ♥ AQJ1075 | | ♥ AJ64 |
| | ♦ K3 | | ♦ 843 |
| | ♣ 942 | | ♣ KJ43 |
| | Rebid 3♥ | | Rebid 2 N.T. |

With the same auction as above, you must place the contract in game having a full opening bid and knowing where the game should be played.

| a) | ♠ K864 | b) | ♠ A4 | c) | ♠ 54 |
|---|---|---|---|---|---|
| | ♥ AQ74 | | ♥ KJ109 | | ♥ AKQJ976 |
| | ♦ A32 | | ♦ Q86 | | ♦ K6 |
| | ♣ 62 | | ♣ A1097 | | ♣ 97 |
| | Rebid 4 ♠ | | Rebid 3 N.T. | | Rebid 4 ♥ |

One of the problems that occurs using a limit system is that often you will not have a forcing bid available.

You hold the following hand: ♠K43 ♥AQ53 ♦A763 ♣97. Again partner opens 1 ♦, you respond 1 ♥, and partner rebids 1 ♠. The forcing bid of 3 ♦ is no longer available, since that would be limit. When this occurs we adopt the principle of fourth-suit forcing. With the above hand you must rebid 2♣ (ALERTABLE), which was always forcing since it is a new suit by responder, but in this case it does not necessarily show a real suit or any stoppers in the suit. It is simply a means to create a forcing auction (usually to game). If opener now rebids no trump, he must have a stopper in the fourth suit.

If partner opens one of a suit, the direct jump to 2 N.T. maintains its standard meaning. It shows an opening bid, stoppers in the unbid suits, and is forcing to game.

Using this system of limit bids requires the discussion of two more bidding sequences.

Partner opens 1 ♣, you respond 1 ♦, and partner rebids one of a major. The jump rebid to 3 ♣ is forcing, showing an opening bid and 4-card or longer club support. This exception is really quite logical. If you had a limit raise in clubs, you would not have taken the time to bid diamonds, the one suit your partner is unlikely to care about. You should simply make the limit raise at your first opportunity to bid.

Partner opens 1♣ and you hold: ♠A4 ♥76 ♦A432 ♣Q10643. Your first response should be 3♣.

Partner opens 1♣, you respond 1♥, and partner rebids 1♠. If you now rebid 3♣, this is a limit raise. Do you see the difference? This time you could not make the limit raise immediately since you hold a 4-card major. When partner fails to support your major, you may then show the full value of your hand by jumping in partner's opened minor.

Partner opens 1♣ and you hold: ♠A4 ♥A432 ♦76 ♣Q10643; you must respond 1♥. If partner now rebids 1♠, you should rebid 3♣, showing a limit raise in clubs and suggesting the possibility of game. Your hand is certainly too good to bid only 2♣.

## *QUIZ #15*

1. Partner opens 1♠. What do you respond with each of the following hands, playing limit raises?

a)    ♠ K875
    ♥ A4
    ♦ KJ4
    ♣ 9732 ____

b)    ♠ K5
    ♥ QJ109
    ♦ AJ7
    ♣ KJ92 ____

c)    ♠ A864
    ♥ A4
    ♦ KQ86
    ♣ 963 ____

d)    ♠ K64
    ♥ K87
    ♦ K432
    ♣ 876 ____

e)    ♠ K64
    ♥ K87
    ♦ KQ43
    ♣ 876 ____

2. Partner opens 1♣. What do you respond with each of the following hands, playing limit raises?

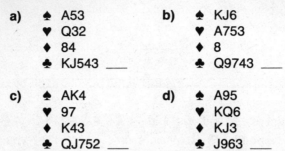

|        |                    |        |                    |
|--------|--------------------|--------|--------------------|
| **a)** | ♠ A53              | **b)** | ♠ KJ6              |
|        | ♥ Q32              |        | ♥ A753             |
|        | ♦ 84               |        | ♦ 8                |
|        | ♣ KJ543 ___        |        | ♣ Q9743 ___        |
|        |                    |        |                    |
| **c)** | ♠ AK4              | **d)** | ♠ A95              |
|        | ♥ 97               |        | ♥ KQ6              |
|        | ♦ K43              |        | ♦ KJ3              |
|        | ♣ QJ752 ___        |        | ♣ J963 ___         |

3. Partner opens 1♦, you respond 1♥, and partner rebids 1♠. What do you rebid with each of the following hands, playing limit raises?

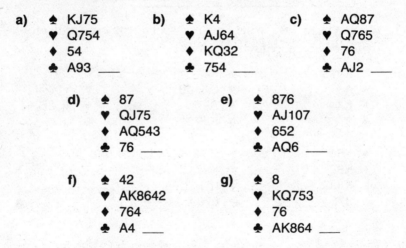

| **a)** | ♠ KJ75 | **b)** | ♠ K4   | **c)** | ♠ AQ87 |
|--------|--------|--------|--------|--------|--------|
|        | ♥ Q754 |        | ♥ AJ64 |        | ♥ Q765 |
|        | ♦ 54   |        | ♦ KQ32 |        | ♦ 76   |
|        | ♣ A93 ___ |     | ♣ 754 ___ |   | ♣ AJ2 ___ |

| **d)** | ♠ 87    | **e)** | ♠ 876   |
|--------|---------|--------|---------|
|        | ♥ QJ75  |        | ♥ AJ107 |
|        | ♦ AQ543 |        | ♦ 652   |
|        | ♣ 76 ___ |       | ♣ AQ6 ___ |

| **f)** | ♠ 42     | **g)** | ♠ 8      |
|--------|----------|--------|----------|
|        | ♥ AK8642 |        | ♥ KQ753  |
|        | ♦ 764    |        | ♦ 76     |
|        | ♣ A4 ___ |        | ♣ AK864 ___ |

# Sixteen

# Michaels

**Purpose:** To show two-suited hands with one bid over an opponent's opening bid of one of a suit.

**Natural Bid Given Up:** The direct cue bid of an opened suit to show a very powerful hand.

**Advantage:** The ability to show a two-suited hand with one bid before the bidding level gets too high.

The cue bid of right-hand opponent's opened minor (ALERTABLE) shows 5–5 in the major suits and 10–13 points. (With a good opening bid and two good suits, it is better to overcall spades and then rebid hearts. This, of course, also shows 5–5, but a better hand.)

Right-hand opponent opens 1 ♣ and you hold the following hands:

| a) | ♠ AQ865 | b) | ♠ 97654 | c) | ♠ AK764 |
|---|---|---|---|---|---|
| | ♥ KJ754 | | ♥ A8754 | | ♥ KQJ86 |
| | ♦ 5 | | ♦ KJ | | ♦ K4 |
| | ♣ 53 | | ♣ Q | | ♣ 5 |
| | Bid 2♣ | | Pass | | Bid 1♠ |

Responding to partner's cue bid of an opponent's opening minor (Michaels) is really quite simple. The response of 2♥ or 2♠ is to play. The response of 3♥ or 3♠ is invitational, asking partner to carry on to game if he is maximum. Bidding game in either major is obviously to play and shows the values for game. The response of 2 N.T. is to play, showing values in the minor suits and denying a fit for either major suit. The response of 3 N.T. is to play and shows stoppers in the minor suits and the values for game.

Left-hand opponent opens 1♦, partner overcalls 2♦, Michaels. Right-hand opponent passes and you hold the following hands:

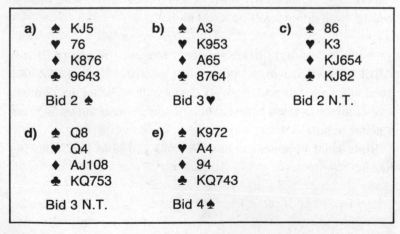

| a) | ♠ KJ5 | b) | ♠ A3 | c) | ♠ 86 |
|---|---|---|---|---|---|
| | ♥ 76 | | ♥ K953 | | ♥ K3 |
| | ♦ K876 | | ♦ A65 | | ♦ KJ654 |
| | ♣ 9643 | | ♣ 8764 | | ♣ KJ82 |
| | Bid 2♠ | | Bid 3♥ | | Bid 2 N.T. |

| d) | ♠ Q8 | e) | ♠ K972 |
|---|---|---|---|
| | ♥ Q4 | | ♥ A4 |
| | ♦ AJ108 | | ♦ 94 |
| | ♣ KQ753 | | ♣ KQ743 |
| | Bid 3 N.T. | | Bid 4♠ |

If right-hand opponent opens a major suit, the cue bid of that major (ALERTABLE) is Michaels, showing five cards in the other major and five cards in an unspecified minor with 10–13 points. Again with two very good suits and a better hand, overcall your major and then bid your minor freely. When cue bidding spades, you should have the upper range, since you are forcing partner to the three-level.

Right-hand opponent opens the bidding 1 ♥ and you hold the following hands:

| a) ♠ AQ975 | b) ♠ Q8753 | c) ♠ KQJ84 |
|---|---|---|
| ♥ 5 | ♥ A5 | ♥ 4 |
| ♦ KQ876 | ♦ K8743 | ♦ 87 |
| ♣ Q3 | ♣ Q | ♣ AKQ87 |
| Bid 2 ♥ | Pass | Bid 1 ♠ |

Responding to partner's cue bid of an opponent's opened major (Michaels) varies from the cue bid of a minor-suit opening. If left-hand opponent opens 1 ♠ and partner bids 2 ♠, the bid of 3 ♥ is to play. If, however, left-hand opponent opens 1 ♥ and partner bids 2 ♥, the response of 2 ♠ is to play. This sequence affords an invitational bid that does not occur when spades is the bid suit. A response of 3 ♥ is invitational, asking the Michaels bidder if he is minimum or maximum. Bidding game in the other major shows the values for game and places the final contract.

If the responder wishes to know which minor the Michaels bidder has, he uses the artificial bid of 2 N.T. (ALERTABLE). This simply asks partner to bid his minor suit. The responder then passes or places the final contract.

Left-hand opponent opens 1 ♥, partner bids 2 ♥, Michaels, and right-hand opponent passes. You hold each of the following hands:

a)  ♠ Q63
    ♥ K742
    ♦ 983
    ♣ 1064

    Bid 2 ♠

b)  ♠ 9
    ♥ QJ106
    ♦ Q432
    ♣ Q873

    Bid 2 N.T.

c)  ♠ J84
    ♥ 63
    ♦ KQ72
    ♣ KQ84

    Bid 3 ♠

d)  ♠ A642
    ♥ 97
    ♦ KJ63
    ♣ KQ4

    Bid 4 ♠

With the strong take-out, you can double and then cue bid the opened suit.

**Basic Defense:** If partner opens and right-hand opponent uses Michaels, the raise of partner's opened suit to the three-level should be nonforcing and show 9–12 points, inviting game. You should bid four of partner's major having the values for game and normal trump support. 2 N.T. shows stoppers in the unbid suits and 9–12 points. A double shows the ability to penalize at least one of the opponents' suits. 3 N.T. is to play, showing stoppers in the unbid suits and the values for game. A cue bid of the opponents' *known* suit shows a good hand (at least an opening bid) and basically asks the opener to describe his hand further. A new suit is natural and forcing.

## *QUIZ #16*

1. Playing Michaels, what do you bid with each of the following hands if right-hand opponent opens 1 ♦ ?

    **a)** ♠ KJ863     **b)** ♠ KQJ94
          ♥ AJ953           ♥ AQJ62
          ♦ Q5           ♦ 9
          ♣ 9 ___           ♣ 106 ___

    **c)** ♠ 107543     **d)** ♠ AQ987
          ♥ 97532           ♥ 74
          ♦ AK           ♦ 8
          ♣ A ___           ♣ KQ1063 ___

2. Left-hand opponent opens 1 ♦ . Partner bids 2 ♦ , Michaels. Right-hand opponent passes. What do you bid with each of the following hands?

**a)** ♠ 95     **b)** ♠ K874     **c)** ♠ Q8
   ♥ 864        ♥ Q8        ♥ Q862
   ♦ KJ32        ♦ 9742        ♦ A76
   ♣ 9743 ___      ♣ AQ8 ___      ♣ KQJ8 ___

**d)** ♠ 73     **e)** ♠ 106
   ♥ A5        ♥ 84
   ♦ KJ82        ♦ AJ109
   ♣ AK532 ___     ♣ KJ964 ___

3. Playing Michaels, what do you bid with each of the following hands if right-hand opponent opens 1 ♥ ?

    **a)** ♠ KJ863     **b)** ♠ AK1092
          ♥ A6           ♥ 9
          ♦ KQ974         ♦ K4
          ♣ 8 ___          ♣ KQ974 ___

    **c)** ♠ 95     **d)** ♠ 108643
          ♥ 4           ♥ AK
          ♦ KQ974        ♦ K9854
          ♣ AKJ86 ___      ♣ Q ___

**4.** Left-hand opponent opens 1 ♥. Partner bids 2 ♥, Michaels. Right-hand opponent passes. What do you bid with each of the following hands?

**a)** ♠ 643
♥ 76
♦ Q964
♣ Q742 ___

**b)** ♠ K876
♥ A3
♦ AJ63
♣ 843 ___

**c)** ♠ K4
♥ QJ109
♦ Q86
♣ AQ74 ___

**d)** ♠ 5
♥ 9854
♦ K754
♣ QJ84 ___

**e)** ♠ A643
♥ 75
♦ AJ74
♣ AQ3 ___

# *Seventeen*

# Negative Doubles

**Purpose:** With the advent of 5-card majors, the heart suit was often lost when partner opened a minor and right-hand opponent overcalled, particularly in spades. The Negative Double was designed to find the heart fit in this situation, although its use has been greatly extended.

**Natural Bid Given Up:** The responder's ability to double low-level overcalls for penalty.

**Advantage:** It is not often that you want to double one- or even two-level contracts for penalty. It is much more important to be able to find fits in suits not yet bid and be able to compete for partials or even find game in these suits.

If partner opens and right-hand opponent overcalls, a double (ALERTABLE) is no longer for penalties. This double actually becomes take-out. The Negative Double shows the other two suits and the inability to make a free bid. In order to make a free bid you need a 5-card suit and/or enough points to bid at the required level. Not having one or the other of these requirements, you use the Negative Double.

Partner opens 1 ♦ , right-hand opponent overcalls 1 ♠ , and you hold:  ♠ 987  ♥ AJ85  ♦ Q4  ♣ Q754. You have no legitimate bid using standard methods. You do not have enough points to bid at the two-level (10 or more), and you certainly do not want to pass. This, of course, is the perfect hand for a Negative Double. The Negative Double in this auction promises four hearts and likely four clubs (the two unbid suits).

There is no point-count restriction for the Negative Double. You may have just enough points (seven or eight) to want to compete to the two-level. You may even have a full opening bid with enough points for game. There is no upper limit.

Partner opens 1 ♦ , right-hand opponent overcalls 1 ♠ , and you hold:  ♠ K3  ♥ QJ987  ♦ Q54  ♣ 973. Although you have a 5-card heart suit, you do not have enough points to bid freely at the two-level. This is another hand for the Negative Double.

Partner opens 1 ♦ , right-hand opponent overcalls 1 ♠ , and you hold:  ♠ 87  ♥ KQ87  ♦ K76  ♣ AJ42. You have more than enough points to bid at the two-level, but to bid a new suit shows at least five cards. Once again the Negative Double. Of course, with this hand you will bid to game once a fit is found.

After using the Negative Double, the principle of responder bidding once with 6–9 points, and twice freely—under game and nonforcing with 10–12 points, and to game with 13 or more points—still holds true.

Partner opens 1 ♦ , right-hand opponent overcalls 1 ♠ , and with each of the following hands, you make a Negative Double. Left-hand opponent passes, partner rebids 2 ♥ , and right-hand opponent passes.

| a) | ♠ 64 | b) | ♠ 64 | c) | ♠ 64 |
|----|------|----|------|----|------|
|    | ♥ KJ76 |  | ♥ AK65 |  | ♥ AK65 |
|    | ♦ K43 |   | ♦ K54 |   | ♦ K54 |
|    | ♣ J532 |  | ♣ J532 |  | ♣ A532 |
|    | Pass |   | Rebid 3♥ | | Rebid 4♥ |

So far, all the examples have partner opening 1♦ and right-hand opponent overcalling 1♠. There are many other sequences where you can use the Negative Double.

• If partner opens 1♣ and right-hand opponent overcalls 1♦, double (Negative) shows at least 4–3 in the major suits. Again the Negative Double shows the two unbid suits.

An exception occurs when partner opens 1♣ and right-hand opponent overcalls 1♦. The response of one of a major may be made on a 4-card suit, implying less than three cards in the other major; otherwise, a Negative Double would be made.

• If partner opens 1♥ and right-hand opponent overcalls 1♠, double (Negative) shows 4–4 in the minor suits.

• If partner opens 1♥ and right-hand opponent overcalls 2♣ or 2♦, double (Negative) shows four spades and the unbid minor.

• If partner opens 1♠ and right-hand opponent overcalls 2♥, double (Negative) shows at least 4–4 in the minor suits.

I suggest that you play Negative Doubles through 2♠ for starters. You may later wish to increase this level. This simply means that all doubles are negative after right-hand opponent overcalls up to and including 2♠. If he overcalls at a higher level than 2♠, then all doubles revert to penalty.

Negative Doubles can also be used to show a weakish one-suited hand with which you are willing to compete but have no interest in game.

Partner opens 1 ♦ , right-hand opponent overcalls 2 ♣ , and you hold: ♠ AQ9765 ♥ 76 ♦ 86 ♣ 853. You cannot bid 2 ♠ freely—not enough points—but you would like to compete for a spade partial. You double (Negative), showing hearts and spades, the two unbid suits. If partner now rebids 2 ♥ , you, of course, will bid 2 ♠ . Something's up. If you had hearts, as advertised, you certainly would not now bid spades. Therefore, you must have long spades with not enough points to have bid freely at your first opportunity to bid. This suggests that the opener pass and allow you to play in 2 ♠ .

Since we lose the ability to double foolish low-level overcalls, the opener is duty-bound to reopen the bidding with a double if he suspects that partner might have wished to double an opponent's overcall for penalty. You should suspect this situation whenever you have extreme shortness in the overcalled suit.

You open 1 ♦ , left-hand opponent overcalls 1 ♠ , partner and right-hand opponent pass, and you hold: ♠ 5 ♥ KQ87 ♦ AJ76 ♣ K743. You should reopen with a double (take-out), but don't be surprised if partner passes for penalty. This, of course, is a textbook hand for reopening with a double.

With the same auction as above, you should also reopen with a double with each of the following hands:

| a) | | b) | |
|---|---|---|---|
| ♠ | 98 | ♠ | 743 |
| ♥ | KJ6 | ♥ | A4 |
| ♦ | AQ865 | ♦ | KQ73 |
| ♣ | K94 | ♣ | A973 |

Remember, the responder must pass holding the overcalled suit hoping that partner will reopen with a double that he can pass, converting to penalty.

## *QUIZ #17*

**1.** Partner opens 1♣, right-hand opponent overcalls 1♠. Playing Negative Doubles, what do you bid with each of the following hands?

**a)** ♠ KJ4
♥ QJ8
♦ K765
♣ 763 ___

**b)** ♠ 865
♥ QJ85
♦ KJ54
♣ Q3 ___

**c)** ♠ AQJ65
♥ 76
♦ K75
♣ 654 ___

**d)** ♠ 7
♥ AQ876
♦ KJ4
♣ QJ53 ___

**e)** ♠ 9
♥ KQJ7654
♦ 542
♣ 65 ___

# *Eighteen*

# Responsive Doubles

**Purpose:**   To eliminate the need to guess what suit to bid when partner makes a take-out double after left-hand opponent opens the bidding and right-hand opponent raises opener's suit to the two- or three-level.

**Natural Bid Given Up:**   The ability to double, for penalty, when partner makes a take-out double and right-hand opponent raises opener's suit.

**Advantage:**   It is rare that you want to make a penalty double of an opened and raised suit at a low level. Therefore, the use of the Responsive Double allows the take-out doubler to choose the suit in which to compete.

If left-hand opponent opens the bidding, partner doubles, and right-hand opponent raises the opener's suit, a double (ALERT-ABLE) by you is no longer for penalty but responsive (which simply means take-out).

When responding to partner's take-out double you usually respond in your longest suit. When right-hand opponent raises opener's suit, you may use the Responsive Double to show length in more than one suit, allowing the take-out doubler to make the decision since his exact distribution is unknown.

Let's look at each of the Responsive Double possibilities separately.

**1.  1♣—X—2♣—or**
   **1♦ —X —2♦ —?**

a) X (the symbol used to indicate a double) shows 4–4 in the majors and 6–12 points. (This eliminates your need to guess which major to bid. Partner will bid his 4-card major, enabling your side to find its 8-card fit.)

b) 3♣ or 3♦, respectively—4–4 in the majors and 13 points. (This asks partner to bid game in his 4-card major.)

c) 2♥ or 2♠—a 4-card suit and 6–9 points.

d) 3♥ or 3♠—a 4-card suit and 10–12 points.

e) 4♥ or 4♠—a 4-card suit and 13 points.

f) 2 N.T.—10–12 points and the opened suit stopped.

g) 3 N.T.—13 points and the opened suit stopped.

**2.  1♥—X—2♥—?**

a) X—denies four spades. Shows four clubs and four diamonds with 8–12 points. (Since spades is the only major partner is interested in, you should bid them with four pieces and the room to bid at the two-level.)

b) 2♠—4-card suit and 6–9 points.

c) 3♠—4-card suit and 10–12 points.

d) 4♠—13 points and a 4-card suit.

e) 3♣ or 3♦—10–12 points, at least a 5-card suit, and is nonforcing.

f) 3♥—game interest in the minors, 13 points.

g) 4♣ or 4♦ —at least a 5-card suit with 13 points. Game interest but nonforcing.

h) 2 N.T.—10–12 points with opened suit stopped.

i) 3 N.T.—13 points with the opened suit stopped.

**3. 1♠—X—2♠—?**

a) X—shows four hearts with less than 10 points. (Since hearts
is the only major partner is interested in, the responsive double shows four of them since you are forced to bid at the
three-level and may not have enough points.)

b) 3♥ —4-card suit with 10–12 points.

c) 4♥ —4-card suit and 13 points.

d) 3♣ or 3♦ —at least a 5-card suit with 10–12 points and
nonforcing.

e) 3♠ —game interest in the minors, 13 points.

f) 4♣ or 4♦ —at least a 5-card suit with 13 points. Game interest but nonforcing.

g) 2 N.T.—10–12 points with the opened suit stopped.

h) 3 N.T.—13 points with the opened suit stopped.

**4. 1♣—X—3♣ or
1♦—X—3♦—?**

a) X—at least 4–3 in the major suits with less than 10 points.

b) 4♣ or 4♦, respectively—4–4 in the majors with 13 points.

c) 3♥ or 3♠ —4-card suit and 10–12 points.

d) 4♥ or 4♠—4-card suit and 13 points.

e) 3 N.T.—13 points with the opened suit stopped.

**5. 1♥—X—3♥—?**

a) X—four spades and less than 10 points.

b) 3♠ —4-card suit and 10–12 points.

c) 4♠ —4-card suit and 13 points.

d) 4♥ —game take-out in the minors.

e) 4♣ or 4♦ —at least a 5-card suit with 13 points. Invitational.

f) 3 N.T.—13 points with the opened suit stopped.

We stop here since I suggest, for the time being anyway, that if you adopt Responsive Doubles, you play them through 3 ♥. If left-hand opponent opens, partner doubles, and right-hand opponent raises opener's suit at a level higher than 3 ♥, a double by you reverts to penalty.

## QUIZ #18

**1.** Left-hand opponent opens 1 ♦, partner doubles, and right-hand opponent bids 2 ♦. Playing Responsive Doubles, what do you bid with each of the following hands?

a)   ♠ K875      b)   ♠ QJ87      c)   ♠ KJ84
      ♥ AQ63           ♥ 65             ♥ QJ65
      ♦ 65             ♦ KQ32       ♦ A743
      ♣ 742 ___       ♣ 972 ___      ♣ 6 ___

      d)   ♠ A4          e)   ♠ AKQ7
          ♥ KQ83         ♥ K5
          ♦ 743           ♦ 8765
          ♣ Q743 ___     ♣ Q84 ___

      f)   ♠ 876        g)   ♠ Q6
         ♥ Q75          ♥ 865
         ♦ KJ75        ♦ AJ10
         ♣ AK5 ___      ♣ K6532 ___

**2.** Left-hand opponent opens 1♥, partner doubles, and right-hand opponent bids 2♥. Playing Responsive Doubles, what do you bid with each of the following hands?

a)  ♠ AJ84
    ♥ 54
    ♦ KQ74
    ♣ 853 ___

b)  ♠ Q76
    ♥ 86
    ♦ KJ53
    ♣ KQ92 ___

c)  ♠ K3
    ♥ 743
    ♦ AQJ865
    ♣ 93 ___

d)  ♠ A1086
    ♥ 65
    ♦ AJ64
    ♣ 853 ___

e)  ♠ A6
    ♥ 932
    ♦ KQ86
    ♣ A987 ___

f)  ♠ KJ84
    ♥ A54
    ♦ AJ4
    ♣ 743 ___

g)  ♠ 1053
    ♥ AQ4
    ♦ K654
    ♣ Q63 ___

h)  ♠ A3
    ♥ 965
    ♦ 865
    ♣ AKQ83 ___

i)  ♠ 765
    ♥ KQ10
    ♦ KJ75
    ♣ A74 ___

**3.** Left-hand opponent opens 1♠, partner doubles, and right-hand opponent bids 2♠. Playing Responsive Doubles, what do you bid with each of the following hands?

a)  ♠ A4
    ♥ KQ87
    ♦ 7543
    ♣ A43 ___

b)  ♠ AK3
    ♥ 754
    ♦ Q654
    ♣ Q43 ___

c)  ♠ 976
    ♥ AJ63
    ♦ AJ3
    ♣ 742 ___

d)  ♠ 54
    ♥ A3
    ♦ 865
    ♣ AKJ975 ___

e)  ♠ 1054
    ♥ KQ75
    ♦ K432
    ♣ 54 ___

f)  ♠ 743
    ♥ Q3
    ♦ KQJ106
    ♣ K73 ___

g)  ♠ 54
    ♥ K32
    ♦ AQ64
    ♣ KJ53 ___

h)  ♠ QJ109
    ♥ K4
    ♦ KJ54
    ♣ A53 ___

**4.** Left-hand opponent opens 1♣, partner doubles, and right-hand opponent bids 3♣. Playing Responsive Doubles, what do you bid with each of the following hands?

a)
♠ AQ65
♥ 76
♦ A543
♣ 874 ___

b)
♠ Q765
♥ K654
♦ A65
♣ 54 ___

c)
♠ K43
♥ Q42
♦ K432
♣ AJ10 ___

d)
♠ KJ93
♥ QJ75
♦ AQ3
♣ 93 ___

e)
♠ A3
♥ AQ84
♦ K432
♣ 862 ___

**5.** Left-hand opponent opens 1♥, partner doubles, and right-hand opponent bids 3♥. Playing Responsive Doubles, what do you bid with each of the following hands?

a)
♠ 43
♥ 5
♦ AQ863
♣ AQ972 ___

b)
♠ 976
♥ AQ
♦ K854
♣ KJ63 ___

c)
♠ QJ75
♥ 43
♦ KJ43
♣ Q72 ___

d)
♠ 9743
♥ 653
♦ AK3
♣ AQ3 ___

e)
♠ KQ53
♥ 65
♦ KQ54
♣ 743 ___

f)
♠ K3
♥ A32
♦ 43
♣ AQ9753 ___

# *Nineteen*

# Roman Key Card Blackwood

**Purpose:** To find out about the trump king when interested in bidding a slam.

**Natural Bid Given Up:** Standard responses to Blackwood.

**Advantage:** To be able to stay out of slam, missing either two aces or an ace and the king of the trump suit. You can also find out whether partner has the trump queen.

After an agreement of suit, the bid of 4 N.T. begins Key Card Blackwood. This bid asks partner about his Key Card holding. The Key Cards are the four aces and the king of the agreed-upon trump suit. Therefore, there are five Key Cards.

If partner bids 4 N.T., Key Card Blackwood, you respond as follows:

> 5 ♣ with 0 or 3 Key Cards
> 5 ♦ with 1 or 4 Key Cards
> 5 ♥ with 2 or 5 Key Cards, without the trump queen
> 5 ♠ with 2 or 5 Key Cards, with the trump queen

If the responder responds in a minor suit, the bid of the next higher suit, other than the agreed-upon trump suit, asks whether the responder has the trump queen.

Without the trump queen, the responder then bids the next higher suit. With the trump queen, the responder skips a suit.

Partner opens 1 ♠ and you respond 3 ♠, forcing. Partner now bids 4 N.T. and you answer 5 ♣, showing 0 or 3 Key Cards. Partner now bids 5 ♦, asking about the spade queen. You hold each of the following hands:

|  | | | |
|---|---|---|---|
| **a)** | ♠ K843 | **b)** | ♠ KQ43 |
| | ♥ A64 | | ♥ A64 |
| | ♦ A763 | | ♦ A763 |
| | ♣ Q3 | | ♣ 87 |

|  |  |
|---|---|
| Respond 5 ♥, | Respond 5 ♠, |
| denying | showing |
| the trump Q | the trump Q |

After 4 N.T., if the Blackwood bidder rebids 5 N.T., he is asking for kings. You respond as in standard Blackwood excluding the trump king. There are now only three kings in question, since the trump king was included as a Key Card.

If the trump suit is clubs, reverse the Key Card responses. 5 ♣ shows 1 or 4 and 5 ♦ shows 3 controls. You are unlikely to have 0 controls; if so, you are already too high.

Here is a guide to determining the Key Card suit:

1. 1 ♣—1 ♥     The raised suit, hearts, is the Key Card suit.
   3 ♥—4 N.T.

2. 1 ♥—2 ♦     With two suits supported, the last raised
   3 ♦—3 ♥     suit, hearts, is the Key Card suit.
   4 N.T.

3.  1♣—2♠     If the responder jump shifts and then bids
    3♦—4 N.T.  Blackwood, the responder's suit, spades, is
              the Key Card suit.

4.  1♦—1♠     A jump rebid suit, spades, is the Key Card
    2♦—3♠     suit.
    4♣—4 N.T.

5.  1♣—1♦     If none of the above exists, the last natural
    1♥—4 N.T.  bid made by the partnership, hearts, is the
              Key Card suit.

## QUIZ #19

1. Partner opens 1♥ and with each of the following hands you
   respond 3♥, forcing. Playing Key Card Blackwood, what do
   you respond if partner bids 4 N.T.?

   a)  ♠ KQ43        b)  ♠ A643
       ♥ A754            ♥ K543
       ♦ A5              ♦ 65
       ♣ 754 ___         ♣ AQ4 ___

   c)  ♠ QJ65        d)  ♠ AJ54
       ♥ KQ53            ♥ Q943
       ♦ KQ4             ♦ AJ6
       ♣ 84 ___          ♣ J4 ___

# Twenty

# Splinters

**Purpose:**   To pinpoint a worthless singleton or void in support of partner's opened major suit when holding an opening bid.

**Natural Bid Given Up:**   None. This is certainly a good argument for adopting splinters.

**Advantage:**   To be able to show partner at least 4-card support for his major, extreme shortness in a particular suit, and announce where your high-card points lie.

After partner opens a major suit, the double jump in another suit (ALERTABLE) shows a *worthless* singleton or void in that suit, 4-card support, and a full opening bid with at least 11 high-card points. You should not splinter with a singleton ace or king so that partner will know that all your high-card points exist in the other three suits. This will enable him to diagnose many marginal slams (lacking in high-card points) knowing that all honors are working. All splinter bids are shown at the four-level, except one. If partner opens 1 ♠, you must bid 4 ♣, 4 ♦, or 4 ♥ to show the singleton or void. If partner opens 1 ♥, the responses of 4 ♣ or 4 ♦ are splinters, but 3 ♠ is a double jump and is a splinter.

Partner opens 1 ♥, right-hand opponent passes, and you hold each of the following hands:

| a) | ♠ K432 | b) | ♠ 9 | c) | ♠ 987 |
|---|---|---|---|---|---|
| | ♥ QJ75 | | ♥ KJ76 | | ♥ AQ76 |
| | ♦ 9 | | ♦ A7652 | | ♦ KJ763 |
| | ♣ AK64 | | ♣ A95 | | ♣ A |
| | Respond 4 ♦ | | Respond 3 ♠ | | Respond 2 ♦ —do not splinter with a singleton ace |

The opener may also splinter. If after opening one of a minor, partner responds 1 of a major, the double jump in another suit (ALERTABLE) by opener is a splinter. This shows a singleton or void in the splintered suit, 4-card support for responder's major, and 20 points, including distribution. This time the responder can evaluate slam possibilities knowing where opener's high-card points lie.

With the following hand: ♠3 ♥AK76 ♦AQ65 ♣AJ64 you open 1 ♦. Partner responds 1 ♥. Rebid 3 ♠.

Another useful bid exists after opening one of a minor if partner responds in a major for which you have 4-card support and 20 points, including distribution. The jump rebid to four of the opened minor (ALERTABLE) shows 4-card support for responder's major, 20 points, and a *solid* 6-card minor. Responder then knows that opener has only three cards in the other two suits and can evaluate slam possibilities knowing there is a solid 6-card suit to provide discards.

With the following hand: ♠4 ♥AK94 ♦AKQ754 ♣42 you open 1 ♦. Partner responds 1 ♥. Rebid 4 ♦.

## QUIZ #20

1. Partner opens 1♥. Playing splinters, what do you respond with each of the following hands?

a) ♠ 9
♥ KJ76
♦ A7653
♣ A73 ___

b) ♠ KQ986
♥ A87
♦ 9
♣ A963 ___

c) ♠ A642
♥ K987
♦ KQ973
♣ — ___

d) ♠ 10
♥ QJ98
♦ K765
♣ Q742 ___

e) ♠ 987
♥ AQ98
♦ A
♣ K10842 ___

f) ♠ 7
♥ QJ54
♦ J108654
♣ 73 ___

2. With each of the following hands, you open 1♣. Partner responds 1♠. Playing splinters, what do you rebid?

a) ♠ KJ94
♥ 5
♦ A4
♣ AKQJ53 ___

b) ♠ AKJ8
♥ A43
♦ 8
♣ AK432 ___

c) ♠ QJ65
♥ AK3
♦ 74
♣ AKQJ ___

d) ♠ AJ65
♥ 9
♦ K763
♣ AQJ9 ___

*Twenty-One*

# Texas Transfers

**Purpose:** To transfer game in the major suits to the 1 or 2 N.T. opening bidder.

**Natural Bid Given Up:** The bids of 4 ♥ or 4 ♠ to play—but, in effect, these bids are still available.

**Advantage:** Texas allows the big hand—the no trump opener —to be the declarer. The weaker hand becomes dummy, allowing the opening lead to come into the stronger hand.

If partner opens 1 or 2 N.T., the jump response to 4 ♦ (ALERTABLE) is a transfer to 4 ♥, which places the final contract in hearts. In order to make this bid, the responder must have at least a 6-card suit and the desire to play game. The responder passes with no interest in slam, but if he now bids 4 N.T., this is Blackwood, since hearts is the established trump suit.

Partner opens 1 N.T. and you hold the following hand: ♠ 76 ♥ AKJ7654 ♦ 43 ♣ 76. Respond 4 ♦, forcing partner to rebid 4 ♥, which you pass.

If partner opens 1 or 2 N.T., the response of 4 ♥ (ALERTABLE) is a transfer to 4 ♠, which also names the trump suit. The responder again passes with no interest in slam, and 4 N.T. is now Blackwood.

Partner opens 2 N.T. and you hold the following hand: ♠ QJ8654  ♥ 87  ♦ 743  ♣ 94. Respond 4 ♥, forcing partner to rebid 4 ♠, which you now pass.

You use these transfer bids on hands that you would have responded 4 ♥ or 4 ♠ to play.

If you use both Texas and Jacoby, a 2-level major suit transfer followed by a raise to game is a mild slam try.

**Basic Defense:**  As in Jacoby, if left-hand opponent opens 1 or 2 N.T. and right-hand opponent transfers at the four-level (Texas), the bid of 4 N.T. shows the minors. A double shows the suit doubled and the nontouching suit. A cue bid of the responder's known suit shows two suits of the same color.

## *Quiz #21*

1. Partner opens 1 N.T. and right-hand opponent passes. Playing Texas, what do you respond with each of the following hands?

a)  ♠ KJ9632
   ♥ A4
   ♦ 742
   ♣ 82 ___

b)  ♠ 63
   ♥ QJ7432
   ♦ Q85
   ♣ 74 ___

c)  ♠ 74
   ♥ AQJ932
   ♦ 83
   ♣ K42 ___

d)  ♠ AQJ754
   ♥ A6
   ♦ K62
   ♣ 104 ___

# Twenty-Two

# Two-Way Stayman

**Purpose:** To show hands with the values either for game or less than game after partner opens 1 N.T., while looking for the best place to play the hand.

**Natural Bid Given Up:** Two diamonds to play or Jacoby transfers.

**Advantage:** To force to game at the two-level, leaving room to find the best game or slam.

After partner opens 1 N.T., the response of 2♣ is Stayman with less than 10 high-card points. The response of 2♦ (ALERTABLE) is Stayman with 10 or more high-card points and is forcing to game.

Partner opens 1 N.T.:

- Responding 2♥ or 2♠ is to play.

- Responding 3♣ or 3♦ is invitational, asking partner to bid game in no trump with a maximum and a fit. You have a 6-card suit headed either by a KQ or a QJ with an outside king.

- Responding 3 ♥ or 3 ♠ shows a 6-card suit and some interest in slam.

- Responding 2 ♣ is Stayman, asking for a 4-card major with 0–8 points, and is nonforcing. Opener still rebids 2 ♦, not having a 4-card major.

- If opener rebids 2 ♦ after a 2 ♣ response, a rebid of 2 ♥ by responder shows a weak hand with five hearts and four spades. A rebid of 2 ♠ shows at least a 5-card suit and is mildly invitational.

- If opener rebids 2 ♦ after a 2 ♣ response, a rebid by responder of 3 ♥ or 3 ♠ is invitational, usually showing a 6-card suit.

- If opener rebids two of a major after a 2 ♣ response, responder's rebid of three of a minor is a sign-off.

- If after responding 2 ♣ the responder rebids 2 N.T., he shows eight or nine points, inviting 3 N.T.

- If opener rebids a major after a 2 ♣ response, a raise of that major by responder shows eight or nine points and is invitational.

The following are all sequences that start with 2 ♦ and are forcing to game:

- Responding 2 ♦ is Stayman, asking for a 4-card major with 10 or more points and is forcing to game. Opener rebids 2 N.T., not having a 4-card major.

- If opener rebids 2 N.T. after a 2 ♦ response, responder's rebid of three of a major shows a 5-card suit and is forcing.

- If opener rebids 2♥ after a 2♦ response, responder's rebid of 2♠ shows a 5-card suit and is forcing.

- If opener rebids 2♠ after a 2♦ response, responder's rebid of 3♥ shows a 5-card suit and is forcing.

- If opener rebids 2 N.T. after a 2♦ response, responder's rebid of four of a major shows a 6-card suit and is to play.

- If opener rebids two of a major after a 2♦ response, responder's rebid of four of that major is to play.

- If opener rebids two of a major, after a 2♦ response, responder's rebid of three of that major shows bad trump or a relatively balanced hand. This could be a slam try. If opener rebids either 3 N.T. or four of the agreed-upon major, he denies interest in slam. The bid of a new suit by opener would show interest in slam and be a cue bid showing an ace.

- If opener rebids two of a major or 2 N.T. after a 2♦ response, responder's rebid of three of a minor is natural and forcing.

- If opener rebids two of a major after a 2♦ response, responder's rebid of 2 N.T. asks for further description. The opener should first show four-cards in the other major or rebid his major with five of them. Opener could even bid a 4-card minor.

- If after responding 2♦ the responder rebids 3 N.T., that is to play.

Opener's rebids after responder bids 2♦:

- 2♥ or 2♠ shows a 4-card suit.

- Two of a major followed by three of that major shows a 5-card suit.

- 2 N.T. denies a 4-card major.

- Three of a minor shows a reasonably good 5-card suit and better than a minimum opening no trump.

## *QUIZ #22*

1. Partner opens 1 N.T. Playing Two-Way Stayman, what do you respond with each of the following hands?

a) ♠ KJ8765
   ♥ 74
   ♦ 643
   ♣ 108 ___

b) ♠ K4
   ♥ 743
   ♦ QJ9864
   ♣ 53 ___

c) ♠ A4
   ♥ KQJ953
   ♦ K54
   ♣ 92 ___

d) ♠ K8765
   ♥ Q854
   ♦ J4
   ♣ 84 ___

e) ♠ 83
   ♥ AQ7532
   ♦ 43
   ♣ J73 ___

f) ♠ 64
   ♥ Q32
   ♦ 64
   ♣ Q109753 ___

g) ♠ K854
   ♥ Q754
   ♦ A5
   ♣ 754 ___

h) ♠ AQ754
   ♥ K5
   ♦ Q43
   ♣ 753 ___

i) ♠ KJ7654
   ♥ A643
   ♦ 64
   ♣ 4 ___

j) ♠ Q864
   ♥ K65
   ♦ A953
   ♣ K3 ___

k) ♠ A3
   ♥ K764
   ♦ 84
   ♣ KQ1074 ___

l) ♠ K65
   ♥ A543
   ♦ AQ32
   ♣ 74 ___

# *Twenty-Three*

# Unusual No Trump

**Purpose:** To show two-suited hands, usually the minors, as a competitive weapon.

**Natural Bid Given Up:** Basically none, since by definition the use of no trump for take-out is "unusual" and is used when the bid of no trump would have no natural meaning.

**Advantage:** To be able to show both minor suits before the bidding level gets too high, often the case when the opponents are bidding the major suits.

**Disadvantage:** Here I must add a personal note. I have found that the convention is useful when you buy the contract either with the hope of making it or as a sacrifice. If the opponents settle in their natural contract, however, you have tipped your hand as to your unusual distribution, and this may help the declarer locate the missing high cards and count the hand.

If right-hand opponent opens the bidding with one of a major, the jump overcall of 2 N.T. (ALERTABLE) is Unusual, that is, it has no natural meaning, and shows at least 5–5 in the minor suits. Your point count varies depending on the vulnerability.

With favorable vulnerability—the opponents are vulnerable and you are not—you are likely to be suggesting a sacrifice against the opponents' major-suit game. Therefore, you may not have great high-card strength.

With favorable vulnerability, right-hand opponent opens 1 ♥ and you hold: ♠54 ♥7 ♦KJ765 ♣KJ854. Overcall 2 N.T., Unusual.

With unfavorable vulnerability—you are vulnerable and the opponents are not—you should have two good suits suggesting that your side has a minor-suit game.

With unfavorable vulnerability, right-hand opponent opens 1 ♥ and you hold: ♠Q3 ♥8 ♦KQJ76 ♣AQ653. Overcall 2 N.T., Unusual.

With equal vulnerability, you must exercise caution. You should have a fairly good hand, since you really don't know whose hand it is and a doubled set may be too costly.

With equal vulnerability, right-hand opponent opens 1 ♥ and you hold each of the following hands:

| a) | ♠ K4 | b) | ♠ K4 |
|---|---|---|---|
| | ♥ 8 | | ♥ 8 |
| | ♦ J8653 | | ♦ KQ1098 |
| | ♣ QJ643 | | ♣ AJ743 |
| | Pass | | Bid 2 N.T. |

If you are in first position and pass, with left-hand opponent and partner also passing, the overcall of 1 N.T. after right-hand opponent opens a major is Unusual. You cannot have a legitimate no trump opening bid since you are a passed hand. The Unusual

No Trump is apt to be more profitable in this sequence, since partner is marked with some strength and it is as likely to be your hand as it is the opponents'.

After three passes, right-hand opponent opens 1 ♠ and you hold the following hand: ♠ QJ7  ♥ —  ♦ K8643  ♣ AJ942. Overcall 1 N.T., Unusual.

If a minor suit is opened by right-hand opponent, the bid of 2 N.T. (ALERTABLE) is still Unusual. However, there are variations as to its meaning. Some partnerships still play it for the minors, since the opened minor is often short.

Right-hand opponent opens 1 ♣ and you hold the following hand: ♠ 54 ♥ 8 ♦ KJ1096 ♣ AQJ75. Bid 2 N.T. for the minors.

Others agree that it shows the two lower unbid suits. In the latter case, the bid of 2 N.T. after an opening bid of 1 ♣ shows diamonds and hearts.

Right-hand opponent opens 1 ♣ and you hold: ♠ 94 ♥ KQ743 ♦ AJ1065 ♣ 3. Bid 2 N.T., showing the red suits.

If right-hand opponent opens 1 ♦ , 2 N.T. shows clubs and hearts.

Right-hand opponent opens 1 ♦ and you hold: ♠ 83 ♥ AQ864 ♦ 4 ♣ KQ742. Bid 2 N.T.

The interpretation you use requires partnership discussion and agreement.

If right-hand opponent opens a minor, you can use Michaels (see page 81) to show the majors. With spades and a minor, you simply overcall spades, planning to bid your minor later if given the opportunity.

The Unusual No Trump can occur in many other bidding situations, usually by the side that did not open the bidding. It is not expedient to exemplify all the situations, but I will show you some of the more common occurrences.

| South | West | North | East |
|-------|------|-------|------|
| 1 ♠ | Pass | 2 ♠ | Pass |
| Pass | 2 N.T. | | |

West's bid of 2 N.T. is Unusual for the minors. He probably didn't feel his hand was good enough to compete earlier, but now that North/South have shown a willingness to stop and partner is marked with some values, he chose to compete and not sell out to 2 ♠. His hand should look something like this: ♠4 ♥43 ♦K10753 ♣A9853.

| South | West | North | East |
|-------|------|-------|------|
| 1 ♠ | Pass | 3 ♠ (Strong) | 3 N.T. |

West's bid of 3 N.T. is certainly Unusual, since 26 or more points have already been announced by the opponents. West's bid suggests a minor-suit sacrifice (assuming favorable vulnerability) after the opponents bid on to 4 ♠. He may even be hinting at a sacrifice against a slam if bid by North/South. East's hand is likely to look something like this: ♠2 ♥3 ♦KJ7643 ♣K10963.

| South | West | North | East |
|-------|------|-------|------|
| 1 ♥ | Pass | 1 N.T. | 2 N.T. |

East's bid of 2 N.T. is Unusual, since he would double with a strong no trump, suggesting that North/South cannot make their contract. Therefore, he is competing with a two-suited hand.

Let's test your ability to think (not fair, I know!). Suppose in the above auction you now respond 3 ♣ and partner rebids 3 ♦. What is partner's hand? He is two-suited with diamonds and spades. If he were one-suited, he would have simply overcalled his suit. If he had clubs, he would not now bid diamonds. Suppose you had responded 3 ♦ and he rebid 3 ♠. What is partner's hand? Good. He has spades and clubs.

| South | West | North | East |
|-------|------|-------|------|
| 1 N.T. | 2 N.T. | | |

West's bid of 2 N.T. is Unusual for the minors. There are other conventions to show other two-suited hands (see Astro, Cappelletti, and Landy). If West had a strong no trump opening, he would have doubled. West's hand should look something like this: ♠3 ♥52 ♦AQ754 ♣AK532.

Whenever no trump is bid and can have no natural meaning, it is Unusual for the minors or the unbid suits, depending on partnership agreement.

**Basic Defense:**   Double of the Unusual No Trump tends to show a defensive hand with at least the ability to double one of the Unusual No Trumper's announced suits.

## *QUIZ #23*

1. Right-hand opponent opens 1 ♠. Playing Unusual No Trump, what do you bid with each of the following hands?

a) ♠ 7
   ♥ K3
   ♦ QJ1076
   ♣ AQ854 ___

b) ♠ 75
   ♥ 9
   ♦ J9643
   ♣ Q6432 ___

c) ♠ Q3
   ♥ 93
   ♦ AKQ85
   ♣ Q932 ___

# *Twenty-Four*

# Weak Jump Shifts

**Purpose:**   To enable the responder to bid with hands of playing strength not normally strong enough to take action.

**Natural Bid Given Up:**   The strong jump shift by responder showing 19 or more points.

**Advantage:**   To be able to take a preemptive action against the opponents and warn partner, who has opened the bidding, that you have a very weak hand able to play only in your suit.

Standard bidding methods enable us to use the Weak Jump Shift if partner opens the bidding and right-hand opponent doubles. A jump in a new suit is weak and preemptive. Remember, redouble shows a good hand with 10 or more points.

The Weak Jump Shift (ALERTABLE) enables us to make the same bid if right-hand opponent overcalls or passes.

If partner opens the bidding and right-hand opponent passes, the Weak Jump Shift should be reserved for hands not good enough to respond at the one-level. You should have a 6-card suit, or longer, and less than six high-card points.

Partner opens 1♣, right-hand opponent passes, and you hold: ♠KJ8754 ♥75 ♦987 ♣63. Playing Weak Jump Shifts, you should respond 2♠. The playing strength of your hand deserves a bid, but you do not want to force or encourage partner to bid again. He would need a ''monster'' to have a game. With the same hand, you should bid 2♠ if right-hand opponent doubles or overcalls at the one-level.

## QUIZ #24

1. Partner opens 1♣ and right-hand opponent passes. Playing Weak Jump Shifts, what do you bid with each of the following hands?

a)
♠ 63
♥ KJ9754
♦ 543
♣ 93 ___

b)
♠ AQ9865
♥ J43
♦ 85
♣ 62 ___

c)
♠ 832
♥ 765
♦ Q97654
♣ 10 ___

# Twenty-Five

# Weak Two-Bids

**Purpose:** To be able to open hands with which you would not normally be able to take any action.

**Natural Bid Given Up:** The opening of 2♦, 2♥, or 2♠ to show a strong hand, forcing to game.

**Advantage:** To be able to describe a hand with playing strength with one bid and preempt the opponents at the same time.

If adopting Weak Two-Bids, the openings of 2♦, 2♥, or 2♠ are no longer strong. These bids show weakish hands with little defensive strength.

To open a Weak Two-Bid you need a 6-card suit headed by two of the top three honors and 6–11 high-card points. You show a hand not good enough to open one and not distributional enough to open three.

In first or second position you should not have an ace or more than one king outside of the opened suit, and no 4-card major in addition to your 6-card suit.

You are in first position and hold the following hand:

```
♠ AQJ876
♥ 87
♦ Q93
♣ 53

Open 2 ♠
```

In third position, with favorable vulnerability, you may open a Weak Two-Bid with a 6-card suit *not* headed by two of the top three honors. You may also have a 4-card major in the hand, as well as an ace or even two kings outside of the opened suit. You are still required to have 6–11 high-card points.

You are in third position with favorable vulnerability and hold the following hand:

```
♠ Q876
♥ KJ7643
♦ A54
♣ —

Open 2 ♥
```

The most important thing to remember when responding to an opening Weak Two-Bid is that partner has *less* than an opening bid. The opening Weak Two-Bidder shows a hand that will probably take five tricks with his suit as trump. In order to have game you will need to provide the other five tricks. Therefore, you must look at trick-taking ability rather than points. You will obviously need a pretty good hand to make a game.

The jump to four of partner's major shows one of two kinds of hands: either a hand that you think will produce game, or a hand with which you want to further the preempt and make life difficult for the opponents. The latter hand should have good trump support, side-suit shortness, and not too many points (5–9 high-card points).

A raise to three of partner's suit is not invitational, but once again furthers the preempt. This bid shows good trump support, some distributional assets, a singleton or a void, and 10–12 high-card points.

Partner opens 2 ♥ and you hold each of the following hands:

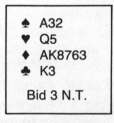

| a) | ♠ AK5 | b) | ♠ 8 | c) | ♠ J976 |
| | ♥ 987 | | ♥ Q874 | | ♥ K876 |
| | ♦ AKQ87 | | ♦ KJ7532 | | ♦ 5 |
| | ♣ 76 | | ♣ 92 | | ♣ AQ92 |
| | Bid 4 ♥ to make | | Bid 4 ♥ preemptive | | Bid 3 ♥ preemptive |

After partner opens a Weak Two-Bid, the jump to 3 N.T. is to play, showing a hand with which you think you can take nine tricks.

Partner opens 2 ♥ and you hold:

```
♠ A32
♥ Q5
♦ AK8763
♣ K3

Bid 3 N.T.
```

A new suit is forcing to the opening two-bidder and specifically asks for support in that suit. If opener has support (three small or an honor doubleton), he raises responder's suit. Not having support, he returns to his opened suit. Therefore, be sure you can tolerate partner rebidding his opened suit.

Partner opens 2♥ and you hold:

```
♠ AQJ765
♥ 74
♦ AQ4
♣ K8

Respond 2♠
```

Responder uses 2 N.T., artificial, when the information about a specific king will help him place the final contract, usually in game in partner's opened major or in 3 N.T.

The bid of 2 N.T. is forcing to opener and asks him to bid a king in an outside suit if he has one. If he has a king, the opener bids three of that suit. Not having a king, he returns to three of his opened suit. (Opener is only permitted to have one king outside of his opened suit.) Again, be sure you can tolerate partner rebidding his opened suit.

Partner opens 2♥ and you hold: ♠K53 ♥87 ♦AQJ765 ♣AK. Respond 2 N.T., and if partner now rebids 3♦, you can rebid 3 N.T. with confidence.

Use forcing bids only when partner has opened a Weak Two-Bid in first or second position and you have a good hand with interest in game.

Since the opening bid of 2♦, 2♥, or 2♠ shows a weak hand, we reserve the opening bid of 2♣ to show all hands with strong two-bids no matter what the suit. The 2♣ bid is artificial, forcing, and simply shows a strong hand to be clarified by the rebid.

With the adoption of Weak Two-Bids, most pairs change their opening bids of 2 N.T. to show 20–22 high-card points and a balanced hand. With 23 or 24 points and a balanced hand, they also open 2♣. Therefore, an opening bid of 2♣ either shows a strong two-bid in a suit, which shows a hand with one trick short of game with your suit as trump, or a balanced hand with 23 or 24 high-card points. Obviously, your rebid will show which hand you have.

You are dealer and hold each of the following hands:

| | |
|---|---|
| ♠ AK | ♠ AQ5 |
| ♥ AQJ876 | ♥ AK6 |
| ♦ A3 | ♦ Q854 |
| ♣ A53 | ♣ AKQ |
| Open 2♣ | Open 2♣ |

If partner opens 2♣, you must think in terms of a positive or negative response. In order to give a positive response, you must meet two requirements. First, you must have at least seven points including an ace, or eight points including a king. Second, to bid a suit you must have at least five cards in that suit. Not having both requirements, you respond 2♦, artificial, which I like to call a *waiting bid*. Your hand may be negative, not having the required point count for a positive response, or you may have a good hand with no 5-card suit to bid. You will certainly let partner know which hand you have after he rebids. Having a positive response with five or more diamonds, you respond 3♦.

Partner opens 2♣ and you hold each of the following hands:

| | |
|---|---|
| ♠ KJ4 | ♠ 94 |
| ♥ AK43 | ♥ 852 |
| ♦ 543 | ♦ KQ10754 |
| ♣ 843 | ♣ A5 |
| Respond 2♦ | Respond 3♦ |
| | |
| ♠ Q8765 | ♠ AQ842 |
| ♥ 65 | ♥ 83 |
| ♦ 865 | ♦ Q53 |
| ♣ J82 | ♣ 862 |
| Respond 2♦ | Respond 2♠ |

Once you've opened 2♣ and partner responds, your rebid shows which of the two kinds of hands you have. If you rebid 2 N.T., you have the balanced hand with 23 or 24 high-card points. If you rebid a suit, you have a strong two-bid in that suit. The rebid of 2 N.T. can be passed, but the rebid of a suit is forcing to game.

Holding each of the following hands, you open 2♣ and partner responds 2♦:

| | |
|---|---|
| ♠ AKQ8765 | ♠ KJ76 |
| ♥ A4 | ♥ AQ5 |
| ♦ AK8 | ♦ AK4 |
| ♣ 6 | ♣ AJ7 |
| Rebid 2♠ | Rebid 2 N.T. |

If the opener rebids 2 N.T. after opening 2♣, the responder is the captain and should know the potential of the hand. He can pass with no points, bid game, or investigate slam.

If you responded 2♦ to partner's 2♣ opening and the opener rebids a suit, you should show support if you have it. Any bid below game is forcing. If opener now bids game, you should pass if your 2♦ bid was, in fact, negative. However, you should bid past game if your 2♦ bid was waiting and you have the required point count for a positive response. Either cue bid an ace, or bid five of partner's major suit, suggesting slam.

If partner opens 2♣, you respond 2♦, and partner rebids a major suit, the jump to game in that major shows a specific hand. You show at least 4-card support, no ace or king, and no singleton or void. You do not have first- or second-round control of any other suit. In other words, the only good feature of your hand is trump length.

Partner opens 2♣ and, holding the following hand, you respond 2♦. Partner rebids 2♥:

> ♠ 876
> ♥ 7643
> ♦ 65
> ♣ 9743
>
> Rebid 4♥

The opening bid of 2♣ can show one other hand. If you adopt Gambling 3 No Trump opening bids (see page 36), then with 25–27 high-card points and a balanced hand, you open 2♣ and rebid 3 N.T.

**Basic Defense:** If right-hand opponent opens a Weak Two-Bid, you pretend he opened one of his suit. If he opens 2♥, you double if you would have doubled an opening bid of 1♥. Overcalling 2 N.T. shows 16–18 points with a balanced hand and at least one stopper in the opened suit. An overcall at the two-level shows a good 5-card suit and at least 10 points. An overcall at the three-level (because your suit is lower-ranking) shows a 6-card suit and practically an opening bid.

## QUIZ #25

1. Playing Weak Two-Bids, what do you open with each of the following hands?

a)
♠ AQ8754
♥ K4
♦ 654
♣ 98 ___

b)
♠ AKQ
♥ AKQ543
♦ A
♣ 864 ___

c)
♠ KJ7654
♥ Q765
♦ 54
♣ K ___

d)
♠ K5
♥ 864
♦ AK7532
♣ 65 ___

e)
♠ AQ5
♥ AKJ
♦ KQJ6
♣ KJ3 ___

f)
♠ 987
♥ Q54
♦ 5
♣ AKJ753 ___

**2.** Partner opens 2 ♥, Weak. What do you respond with each of the following hands?

**a)** ♠ KJ7654
♥ 76
♦ 765
♣ K4 ___

**b)** ♠ AK4
♥ Q876
♦ AK54
♣ 43 ___

**c)** ♠ AQJ643
♥ 98
♦ KQ65
♣ 8 ___

**d)** ♠ A54
♥ Q5
♦ AKQJ10
♣ 643 ___

**e)** ♠ 6
♥ Q765
♦ K765
♣ K954 ___

**3.** Partner opens 2 ♣. What do you respond with each of the following hands?

**a)** ♠ KQ765
♥ K6
♦ 764
♣ 953 ___

**b)** ♠ A765
♥ 876
♦ K65
♣ 543 ___

**c)** ♠ 65
♥ Q97542
♦ J54
♣ 54 ___

**4.** Partner opens 2 ♣. With each of the following hands you respond 2 ♦. What do you rebid if partner rebids 2 N.T.? 2 ♥?

**a)** ♠ 986
♥ Q54
♦ 8754
♣ 753 ___ ___

**b)** ♠ KQ7
♥ 976
♦ K543
♣ 843 ___ ___

**c)** ♠ 87
♥ 8754
♦ Q43
♣ 9743 ___ ___

**d)** ♠ Q98654
♥ 6
♦ 763
♣ 953 ___ ___

**e)** ♠ AK4
♥ 964
♦ KJ32
♣ 843 ___ ___

# *Answers To Quizzes*

## *Quiz #1: Astro*

---

1.  a) 2♦, showing spades and a lower-ranking suit
    b) 2♣, showing hearts and a minor
    c) 2♦, showing spades and a lower-ranking suit
    d) Pass—not good enough to take action
    e) 2♥, natural
    f) 2♣, showing hearts and a minor
    g) 3♦, natural

2.  a) Pass
    b) 2♥
    c) 2 N.T.
    d) 3♥
    e) 2♦
    f) 4♥
    g) 3♣

3.  a) 2♠
    b) Pass
    c) 3♣
    d) 2 N.T.

## *Quiz #2: Cappelletti*

**1.** a) 2♣, showing a one-suited hand
b) 2♦, for the majors
c) 2♥, showing hearts and a minor
d) 2♠, showing spades and a minor
e) 2♣, again a one-suited hand

**2.** a) 1. 2♦ 2. 2♠ 3. Pass 4. Pass
b) 1. 2♦ 2. 2♥ 3. Pass 4. 2 N.T.
c) 1. 2♦ 2. 3♠ 3. Pass 4. 3♠

## *Quiz #3: Dope, Dopi*

**1.** a) double, pass
b) pass, double
c) Pass, 5♦
d) Double, 5♥

## *Quiz #4: Drury*

**1.** a) 2♣
b) 2♣
c) 2♠
d) 4♠—you want to be in game, even if partner opened light.
e) 2♣, planning to rebid 3♣

**2.** a) 2♦
b) 2♥
c) 2♠
d) 2 N.T.
e) 2♦

## *Quiz #5: Flannery 2♦*

1. a) 2♦
   b) 1♠
   c) Pass
   d) 1♥, plan to reverse
   e) 2♦
   f) 1♥, plan to reverse

2. a) 2♠
   b) 4♥
   c) 3♠
   d) 2 N.T., planning to bid slam if partner is short in clubs
   e) 3 N.T.
   f) 4♠
   g) Pass
   h) 2♥, the least of evils

3. a) 3♥
   b) 3♦
   c) 4♦
   d) 3♠
   e) 3 N.T.

4. a) 3♥
   b) Pass
   c) Pass
   d) 4♥
   e) Pass
   f) 3♥
   g) 3♥

5. a) 3♦
   b) 4♣
   c) Pass
   d) 4♠

   e) Pass
   f) 3 ♥
   g) 3 N.T.

## Quiz #6: Forcing No Trump

**1.** a) 1 N.T., followed by 3 ♥
   b) 2 ♥
   c) 3 ♥, limit raise
   d) 1 N.T., planning to pass opener's rebid
   e) 1 N.T., planning to pass 2 ♦ or 2 ♥ and bidding 2 ♦ if opener rebids 2 ♣
   f) 1 N.T., planning to pass 2 ♥ and rebidding 2 ♥ if opener rebids 2 ♣ or 2 ♦
   g) 1 N.T., followed by 2 N.T.
   h) 1 N.T., followed by 2 ♥ if partner rebids a minor. Partner may have a 3-card minor and ace and one is decent support.

**2.** a) 2 ♦
   b) 2 ♥
   c) 2 ♠
   d) 2 ♣
   e) 2 ♠
   f) 2 ♦

## Quiz #7: Gambling 3 No Trump

**1.** a) 3 N.T.
   b) 1 ♣
   c) 1 ♦
   d) 3 ♣—let's not forget a standard preempt.

**2.** a) Pass
   b) 4 ♦ asking for a singleton—let's find that slam.
   c) 4 ♣
   d) 4 ♥
   e) 5 ♣—let's keep them out of game.
   f) Pass
   g) 6 ♣

## Quiz #8: Grand Slam Force

**1.** a) 6 ♦ , showing the Q
   b) 6 ♣ , showing no honor
   c) 6 ♠ , showing five cards to the A
   d) 6 ♥ , showing four cards to the A or K
   e) 7 ♠ , showing two of the top three honors

## Quiz #9: Jacoby Transfers

**1.** a) 2 ♥ , followed by 2 N.T.
   b) 2 ♦ , followed by pass
   c) 2 ♥ , followed by 4 ♠
   d) 2 ♦ , followed by 3 ♥
   e) 2 ♥ , followed by 3 N.T.
   f) 2 ♥ , followed by pass
   g) 2 ♦ , followed by 3 N.T.
   h) 2 ♣ , Stayman
   i) 2 ♦ , followed by 4 ♥
   j) 2 ♥ , followed by 3 ♠
   k) 2 ♠ , minor-suit Stayman with slam interest
   l) 2 ♥ , followed by 3 ♥

m) 2 ♥, followed by 3 ♣, a two-suited slam try

n) 2 ♦, followed by 2 N.T.

o) 2 ♥, followed by 4 ♥, showing 5–5 in the majors

2. a) Pass, Pass

b) 3 ♥, 4 ♥

3. a) 4 ♠, 4 ♠, 4 ♠

b) 3 N.T., Pass, 4 ♥

## Quiz #10: Jacoby 2 No Trump

1. a) 2 ♦

b) 2 N.T.

c) 2 ♣

2. a) 4 ♠

b) 3 ♥

c) 3 ♠

d) 4 ♥

e) 3 N.T.

## Quiz #11: Jordan

1. a) 2 N.T.

b) 1 N.T.

c) 2 ♥

d) 3 ♥

e) Redouble

2. a) 1 ♥

b) 2 N.T.

c) 2 ♦

   d) 3 ♦
   e) Redouble
   f) 1 N.T.

## *Quiz #12: Landy*

**1.** a) 2 ♣
   b) 2 ♣
   c) Pass—not enough strength to take action
   d) 2 ♠
   e) 3 ♣

**2.** a) 2 ♠
   b) 3 ♣
   c) 2 ♥
   d) Pass
   e) 4 ♠
   f) 3 ♥
   g) 2 N.T.
   h) 3 N.T.
   i) 3 ♦
   j) 2 ♦
   k) 4 ♥

## *Quiz #13: Lebensohl Over No Trump*

**1.** a) 2 ♠ , to play
   b) 3 ♥ , Stayman without a stopper
   c) 2 N.T., followed by 3 ♠ , invitational
   d) 2 N.T., followed by 3 ♦ , to play
   e) 3 ♠ , forcing
   f) 3 ♣ , invitational

g) 2 N.T., followed by 3 ♥, Stayman, showing a stopper

h) 3 N.T., no stopper

i) 2 N.T., followed by 3 N.T., showing a stopper

## Quiz #14: Lebensohl Over Weak Two-Bids

1. a) 2 N.T., followed by pass
   b) 2 ♠ to play
   c) 3 ♣, invitational
   d) 2 N.T., followed by 3 ♠ invitational
   e) 3 ♥, forcing
   f) 3 N.T., showing a stopper
   g) 2 N.T., followed by 3 N.T., showing a double-stopper

## Quiz #15: Limit Raises

1. a) 3 ♠, limit
   b) 2 N.T., natural
   c) 3 N.T., forcing raise
   d) 2 ♠
   e) 2 ♦ —you need 4-card support for limit raise.

2. a) 3 ♣, limit
   b) 1 ♥ —you must show a 4-card major first.
   c) 1 ♦, planning to jump in clubs next, forcing
   d) 2 N.T., natural

3. a) 3 ♠, limit
   b) 2 ♣, fourth-suit forcing
   c) 4 ♠
   d) 3 ♦, limit
   e) 2 N.T., limit

ANSWERS TO QUIZZES      133

f) 3♥ , limit
g) 2♣ , planning to rebid 3♣

## Quiz #16: Michaels

1. a) 2♦
   b) 1♠
   c) Pass—two very bad suits
   d) 1♠

2. a) 2♥ , to play
   b) 3♠ , invitational
   c) 4♥
   d) 3 N.T.
   e) 2 N.T.

3. a) 2♥
   b) 1♠
   c) 2♦
   d) Pass

4. a) 2♠
   b) 3♠ , invitational
   c) 3 N.T.
   d) 2 N.T., asking partner to bid his minor suit
   e) 4♠

## Quiz #17: Negative Doubles

1. a) 1 N.T.
   b) Double
   c) Pass
   d) 2♥
   e) Double, followed by bidding hearts to show a weak hand

## *Quiz #18: Responsive Doubles*

1. a) Double
   b) 2 ♠
   c) 3 ♦
   d) 3 ♥
   e) 4 ♠
   f) 3 N.T.
   g) 2 N.T.

2. a) 3 ♠
   b) Double
   c) 3 ♦
   d) 2 ♠
   e) 3 ♥
   f) 4 ♠
   g) 2 N.T.
   h) 4 ♣
   i) 3 N.T.

3. a) 4 ♥
   b) 2 N.T.
   c) 3 ♥
   d) 4 ♣
   e) Double
   f) 3 ♦
   g) 3 ♠
   h) 3 N.T.

4. a) 3 ♠
   b) Double
   c) 3 N.T.
   d) 4 ♣
   e) 4 ♥

**5.** a) 4 ♥
   b) 3 N.T.
   c) Double
   d) 4 ♠
   e) 3 ♠
   f) 3 N.T., you have to take some chances

## Quiz #19: Roman Key Card Blackwood

**1.** a) 5 ♥, showing two Key Cards without the trump Q
   b) 5 ♣, showing 0 or 3 Key Cards
   c) 5 ♦, showing 1 or 4 Key Cards
   d) 5 ♠, showing two Key Cards with the trump Q

## Quiz #20: Splinters

**1.** a) 3 ♠
   b) 1 ♠ —you need 4-card support to splinter
   c) 4 ♣
   d) 4 ♥ —don't forget this bid
   e) 2 ♣ —don't splinter with a singleton ace
   f) 2 ♥ —more than enough

**2.** a) 4 ♣
   b) 4 ♦
   c) 4 ♠
   d) 3 ♠ —not enough to force to game

## Quiz #21: Texas Transfers

**1.** a) 4 ♥
   b) 2 ♥ or 2 ♦, Jacoby, planning to pass 2 ♥

   c) 4 ♦

   d) 3 ♠ —invite slam with this hand

## Quiz #22: Two-Way Stayman

1. a) 2 ♠ , to play
   b) 3 ♦ , invitational
   c) 3 ♥ , forcing
   d) 2 ♣, followed by 2 ♠ if partner rebids 2 ♦
   e) 2 ♣, followed by 3 ♥, invitational
   f) 2 ♣, followed by 3 ♣, sign-off
   g) 2 ♣, followed by 2 N.T. if opener rebids 2 ♦. If opener rebids a major, raise that major to 3. Both bids are invitational.
   h) 2 ♦, followed by 3 ♠ if opener rebids 2 N.T.; 2 ♦, followed by 2 ♠ if opener rebids 2 ♥. Both rebids are forcing, showing a 5-card suit.
   i) 2 ♦, followed by 4 ♠ if opener doesn't bid hearts. Rebid 4 ♥ if opener rebids 2 ♥.
   j) 2 ♦, followed by 3 N.T. if opener rebids 2 ♥. If opener rebids 2 ♠, raise to 3 ♠, showing poor trump and a balanced hand, forcing.
   k) 2 ♦, followed by 3 ♣, natural, and forcing
   l) 2 ♦, followed by 2 N.T., asking for a further description of opener's hand

## Quiz #23: Unusual No Trump

1. a) 2 N.T.
   b) Pass
   c) 2 ♦

## *Quiz #24: Weak Jump Shifts*

1. a) 2 ♥
   b) 1 ♠—too good for a Weak Jump Shift
   c) Pass—the opponents will surely balance

## *Quiz #25: Weak Two-Bids*

1. a) 2 ♠
   b) 2 ♣—strong, artificial, and forcing. You plan to rebid hearts to show a strong two-bid.
   c) Pass
   d) 2 ♦
   e) 2 ♣, followed by 2 N.T.
   f) Pass—there is no weak two-bid in clubs.

2. a) Pass
   b) 4 ♥, to make
   c) 2 ♠
   d) 2 N.T., asking for a king
   e) 4 ♥, preemptive

3. a) 2 ♠, positive
   b) 2 ♦, waiting
   c) 2 ♦, negative

4. a) Pass, 3 ♥
   b) 3 N.T., 3 ♥
   c) Pass, 4 ♥
   d) 4 ♠, 2 ♠
   e) 6 N.T., 3 ♥, planning to bid on to slam